Talented Young Men Overcoming Tough Times

Talented Young Men Overcoming Tough Times

An Exploration of Resilience

Thomas P. Hébert, Ph.D.

Prufrock Press Inc.
Waco, Texas

Library of Congress catalog information currently on file with the publisher.

Copyright ©2018, Prufrock Press Inc.

Edited by Lacy Compton

Cover and layout design by Micah Benson

ISBN-13: 978-1-61821-816-2

No part of this book may be reproduced, translated, stored in a retrieval system, or transmitted, in any form or by any means, electronic, mechanical, photocopying, microfilming, recording, or otherwise, without written permission from the publisher.

For more information about our copyright policy or to request reprint permissions, visit https://www.prufrock.com/permissions.aspx.

Printed in the United States of America.

At the time of this book's publication, all facts and figures cited are the most current available. All telephone numbers, addresses, and website URLs are accurate and active. All publications, organizations, websites, and other resources exist as described in the book, and all have been verified. The authors and Prufrock Press Inc. make no warranty or guarantee concerning the information and materials given out by organizations or content found at websites, and we are not responsible for any changes that occur after this book's publication. If you find an error, please contact Prufrock Press Inc.

Prufrock Press Inc.
P.O. Box 8813
Waco, TX 76714-8813
Phone: (800) 998-2208
Fax: (800) 240-0333
http://www.prufrock.com

Table of Contents

Dedication and Acknowledgments . . . . **vii**

Introduction **1**

Chapter 1: Joseph **5**

Chapter 2: Keith **27**

Chapter 3: Dante **47**

Chapter 4: Sebastian **73**

Chapter 5: Patrick **93**

Conclusion **121**

Afterword **153**

References **155**

About the Author **163**

Dedication

In memory of my father, J. Paul Hébert, whose life continues to provide me inspiration and personal strength.

Acknowledgments

I would like to thank my friend Jean Peterson for her thorough review of my work. Her insights and thoughtful critique helped to strengthen this book. I appreciate her important contributions.

I would like to thank my colleagues in gifted education who introduced me to the five gifted young men presented in this work. These dedicated educators enabled me to conduct my study.

I also want to thank Joel McIntosh and his staff at Prufrock Press, particularly Katy McDowall for her dedication to this project.

I especially want to thank my editor Lacy Compton, who remained committed to this project as we made this journey together.

I am most indebted to the five gifted men who openly shared their lives with me so that we might all learn from them.

INTRODUCTION

University colleagues assured me that my life would change. I had been promoted to the rank of full professor. I had reached the professional stage of my career in higher education when I would no longer have to worry about meeting the expectations of another committee on tenure and promotion. I had made it to the top. I could begin to have fun!

I reflected on a recorded song from the late 1960s that my parents often played on the family's stereo. The renowned American jazz singer Peggy Lee sang "Is That All There Is?" In that tune she described the bewilderment she felt as a young girl when she arrived at a circus and saw clowns and elephants and dancing bears, yet felt that something was missing. She continued to sing about anticlimactic events in life and wrapped up the chorus with "If that's all there is, then I'll keep dancing" (Leiber & Stoller, 1969). I felt the same. I had achieved the final promotion but realized I needed to keep dancing. I searched for new challenges that would keep me intellectually engaged and passionate about my scholarly interests.

I discovered that my university offered a competitive faculty research leave. This program enabled professors to enjoy a mini-sabbatical. The thought of taking time off from the routine of teaching classes and participating in endless committee meetings sounded wonderful. With time away from campus, I could focus on a new research project and become reinvigorated. I submitted my research proposal, and shortly after, I celebrated when I learned I had been granted a semester's leave.

Until that time, my research had explored the social and emotional development of gifted young people, with many of my scholarly manuscripts focused on gifted males. I had also studied intelligent adolescents whose lives beyond school were filled with serious challenges.

I chose to continue this line of inquiry. My new study, which led to this book, would examine the experiences of high-achieving talented males who had overcome serious adversity. I wanted to investigate young men thriving in university life or in the early stages of their professional careers. For this study I would explore two overarching questions. I wanted to understand how these high-achieving gifted males overcame adverse circumstances to reach high levels of achievement. Moreover, I wanted to understand and appreciate the relationships that had guided their behaviors, attitudes, and aspirations.

I turned to my friends in the field of gifted and talented education throughout the country. I asked public school teachers and university educators to nominate young men for my study. I was gratified that so many colleagues were happy to help. They recommended young men they had worked with in their settings and introduced them to me. I was delighted with the diverse group of men who became the subjects for my research.

My colleagues initiated a conversation with each of the individual young men to explore whether they would be willing to participate in the study. When they agreed, I communicated with them via e-mail and described my proposed research. I explained that I would travel to their community and spend a week in their contexts to conduct extensive qualitative interviews with each of them individually. I needed uninterrupted time with them in order to capture their complete life stories. I was able to negotiate a calendar with each of them, and they graciously afforded me the time I needed for the interviews. Once dates were determined, I moved forward with travel plans.

The men in the study had all left their hometowns and were living in various places throughout the country. Although I was meeting them in their new professional contexts, the earlier chapters of their life stories had occurred elsewhere. My travels began in January and lasted through May. In some cases, I was able to travel by car; other experiences involved airline flights and car rentals. Each trip involved some personal anxiety. The thought of traveling to a new community and making connections with the young men I had never met seemed intimidating at first. I wondered, "Would they be open to me?", "Would they like me?", and "Would I be able to develop a comfortable rapport quickly enough?" I also imagined that the men were probably asking similar questions about me.

My colleagues who had recommended the participants were critical to my success. They served as important gatekeepers and opened the way for me to make connections with the men. These educators had assured the men that they would enjoy working with me and that their contributions to this research would be significant. I quickly discovered that I would enjoy my semester working with them. The men were delightful to work with. Although they had difficult stories to share with me, I realized that the experience was likely therapeutic for them. I believe that their involvement in my research also served as validation for their having created successful, meaningful lives. Through this work, I made significant new friendships, and I remain connected to each of them today. This book features the life stories of five intelligent young men who have important experiences to share with us. I present each of them to you in separate chapters. The concluding chapter presents my thematic analysis of the findings from this study and highlights the scholarly literature to reinforce their significance.

I have selected five representative stories for this book. I will introduce you to Joseph, Keith, Dante, Sebastian, and Patrick. Their stories are compelling and involve adversity that is not at all pleasant. Some of these stories involve similar kinds of adversity. To protect the identities of the young men and their families, pseudonyms are incorporated throughout the book. I am honored that they imparted their life experiences to me, and I humbly pass them on to you. There are important lessons that we learn from these strong, impressive, and inspiring individuals.

CHAPTER 1

JOSEPH

Joseph Ideye was a sophomore at a large research university in New England, enjoying his winter holiday break between semesters. He greeted me with an authentic smile as he walked through the door of his university library. Dressed in cargo style jeans, a university sweatshirt, a heavy parka, and a woolen scarf, Joseph was clearly accustomed to the cold winter weather in New England. This young Black gentleman maintained a rugged athletic physique and appeared self-assured and outgoing. We agreed that a private conference room in the library would be ideal for conducting our interviews, and we succeeded in locating a quiet room for our conversations.

My interviews with Joseph took place during a significant time in our country. We were anticipating the first inauguration of Barack Obama. During the presidential campaign, Americans had come to know the complicated biography of their first African American president and were aware of the significance of President Obama's relationship with his father. I had looked forward to interviewing Joseph because I knew that I would learn so much from him. What I did not realize at that time was that I would later draw comparisons to our president's early years.

Joseph's story is that of a multitalented young man with a complex family history. Having overcome difficult family challenges and homelessness during his adolescence, he was now enjoying a more sedate time in his life as he immersed himself in the college experience.

Joseph's Early Childhood and Elementary School Years

Joseph arrived in the world 3 months premature, an infant tiny enough to be cradled in his father's hand. He was born in a large urban community in the South to a mother addicted to drugs and a father who worked seriously to acquire help for his troubled wife. Joseph's father had left Nigeria and come to the United States on a student visa. Having been educated in boarding schools in Nigeria, he was sent to study mathematics at a small private liberal arts college and eventually earned a master's degree from the University of Arkansas at Little Rock. While on vacation from school, he traveled to a neighboring state, where he met Joseph's mother. Following a short courtship, the couple married and remained near the bride's extended family.

When Joseph was born, his mother insisted on naming him Juniper Joseph Ideye. His father later recounted that his mother enjoyed juniper as a fragrance and decided that it would serve as a beautiful name for her child. He explained, "She really liked the name and didn't care whether I was a boy or girl, dog or cat. She liked the name and that was it." He continued, "Since my father was from Nigeria, he didn't see any problems with the name, and no one in the family looked at this as gender-specific." Later, Joseph resented the teasing he had to endure from his peers on the school playground when they questioned him as to why he had a feminine name. By seventh grade, he insisted on being called Joseph.

The Ideyes' marriage became troubled, and the couple separated when Joseph was 2 years old. His mother's drug addiction had worsened, and his father succeeded in acquiring custody of his son. Mr. Ideye and Joseph remained in their urban community. Joseph's earliest memories of those years included forming strong bonds with a family who lived in the same apartment complex. A single mother with four children became the maternal influence in Joseph's early childhood. Maria Basurto's children became "adopted siblings" for Joseph, while Mr. Ideye became the mentoring role model for her children. Joseph explained, "These two single parents supported each other as they shared the parenting roles." Joseph smiled as he reflected on his relationship with this family. He explained, "I'm still in touch with them. I call them every once in a while, and I'm on Facebook with them. As for Maria, it's the same connection that one might have with a biological mother."

Joseph's pleasant memories of school centered on his first-grade teacher, who worked closely with his father in developing patience with his lively, talkative son who was often scolded for being disruptive. He explained, "She really tried to work with me, often cutting me some slack. I think she liked my dad and understood how much he was juggling as a single parent and how that might have been affecting me." Coming from Nigeria where education was highly valued, Mr. Ideye became frustrated as he struggled to understand his son's response to school. Joseph reflected on his father's view of schooling: "Nigerians look to America as God's garden of Eden. They see nothing but opportunity, and getting an education in the United States means you return to Nigeria with knowledge." Fortunately, Joseph's teachers understood the cultural differences Mr. Ideye was not appreciating and provided guidance to him for working with his son. Joseph described how this scenario continued:

> I've always been a kid of questions. I asked a thousand and two questions about everything that was going on to make sure I understood. All of my teachers were saying pretty much the same thing. "He's a very smart. He's very bright, but at the same time, he's disruptive and has trouble sitting down." It was like they loved me, but I drove them crazy at the same time. This pattern of trouble in school lasted all through my elementary school years.

Joseph's father had difficulty finding employment. Although he had earned a graduate degree in mathematics, without American citizenship he was not able to acquire positions for which he was qualified. To survive financially, he was forced to accept jobs in the dry cleaning industry. Frustrated with the lack of opportunities in the South, he decided to move to New England in search of employment. He and Joseph moved in with extended family members who had immigrated to the United States and were living in a New England suburb. They lived with Joseph's aunt and uncle for a year before moving to a neighboring city. As a 7-year-old, Joseph's transition was difficult. "I remember sobbing when we left the Basurtos. My father kept assuring me that things would be okay." Anxiously, he realized he would live with members of his "actual bloodline family" whom he had never known of prior to the move. He struggled to appreciate his new surroundings: "I didn't like anything in the North because it wasn't home. In school I had two strikes against me. I spoke with a Southern accent, and I got teased because I had a girl's name."

Living in a Nigerian household involved culture shock for Joseph. He described being exposed to new foods, learning new ways of conducting oneself with elders, and being intrigued with the Nigerian social events in which families wore African attire complete with elaborate and colorful headdresses. He chuckled as he shared his reflections:

> It was a whole new culture for me. Everything from consistent bedtime to "This is how we do things in this household." It was a big change. . . . They enjoyed brown beans and plantains. I grew up on Popeye's and Church's Chicken, and they'd never had that [laughs]. Everything was so different.

Joseph and his father moved to a large urban community as he entered third grade. His father had again acquired work in a dry cleaning establishment and they moved into an apartment of their own. He described his new home: "It was an unsafe neighborhood. You didn't know your neighbors, so my dad restricted me to be within the fence of the complex we lived in. I never actually ventured off and explored. I was confined to the quarters." Joseph understood why his father was being protective, and he learned that he needed to return home directly after school, lock the door of the apartment, and complete his homework. As a result of this independence at home, he learned to cook for himself: "I needed to be able to fend for myself until dad got home. My father would leave sandwich meats, and I'd make sandwiches, but that got old, so the first thing I learned to cook was macaroni and cheese." As a self-sufficient college student, he appreciated that he had developed these skills. He pointed out that Nigerian families maintained expectations for children whereby they were responsible to care for younger siblings and their elders. He indicated, "My father taught me how to do things. In third grade, I was responsible for cleaning up and making sure the apartment was neat. I couldn't just leave it for Dad. That was my job."

In fourth grade, a friend of the Ideye family introduced Joseph to her church and invited him to join the African American congregation for Sunday worship services at First Baptist. Joseph made connections with other families who were happy to provide him transportation to and from Sunday services. The church had begun a small private Christian school, and Joseph's father was happy to enroll his son in this new setting. Although Mr. Ideye was struggling financially, the school administration was willing to negotiate a reduced tuition rate. Joseph indicated he appreciated that the school instituted a school uniform, which served as an important equalizer for low-income students and made his life easier. He thrived in this more intimate environment under the tutelage of Mrs. Wilson, his fourth- and fifth-grade teacher. He described their relationship:

> I don't want to say that she adopted me, but she spent a lot of time investigating what was going on in my life. She'd start conversations with "How are you doing?", "What's going on?", "How's life?" This was the first time I really connected with one of my teachers. We used to spend a lot of time together talking. She even brought me with her to visit her family in Norfolk, VA. We went to the aquarium, and I got to see the beach. It was really cool. When my father's hours at work changed, she would come to my house and take me to school.

Joseph became more involved in the church and enjoyed faith-based conversations with other students from the congregation as they negotiated the challenges of early adolescence and attempted to build "a good Christian foundation." In this setting, he felt comfortable sharing his insights regarding cultural differences between his Nigerian family and what he experienced in his community. When his father faced more financial difficulties, the school administrators decided that they could no longer waive tuition for him, and Joseph was forced to return to the public schools. Fortunately, the local system had established a sixth-grade science and math magnet school, and through the luck of a lottery system, Joseph was able to enroll in this new program. He enjoyed the curricular focus on science and exposure to Japanese language and culture. His first experience with a male teacher also proved to be significant. There, he connected with Paul Gagliano, a young sixth-grade teacher who took a sincere interest in Joseph's well-being, spent time discussing sports with him, provided guidance in how to negotiate peer relationships, and brought the outside world into his daily curriculum. Mr. Gagliano also selected him for a leading role in a small class play, entitled "We Have Jazz," about a young man who comes to appreciate music when he learns about rhythm and blues and the history of jazz through Ella Fitzgerald's story. In this setting, Joseph formed what he called "real trusting friendships" with two other boys—they became a well-known trio in that school and have remained good friends since.

Joseph's Middle and High School Years

Joseph's middle school was a student body of 1,200 seventh and eighth graders—organized in several teams with specific faculty members assigned to each team. Joseph described his identity search during this period as a time of figuring out "Who am I, and where do I stand?" He decided he was neither "the ghetto type" and did not want to be associated with that group, nor was he one of the "brainiacs." He confessed that he saw himself as one of the "cool ones" who did not dedicate enough energy to academics, and he described incidents in which he was disciplined for being disrespectful to teachers and skipping classes. His father was very concerned and wondered if the presence of a new girlfriend in his life was causing his son to rebel. His father's girlfriend only exacerbated the situation when she talked about "getting his act together," and his father's comparisons to his Nigerian "honor roll cousins" did not improve the situation.

A significant teacher intervened and helped to turn things around. Joseph's team teachers had decided that they wanted him transferred to another team and were considering whether to recommend him to an alternative school in the district. John Hannigan, the team's English teacher and drama coach, apparently saw Joseph's potential and insisted that they continue working with him. Mr. Hannigan shared with Joseph how he had gone to bat for him when all others had given up on him. Because Joseph had been disrespectful to Mr. Hannigan, he was stunned and quickly changed his behavior. Joseph described this "a critical turning point in my academic career." He joined Mr. Hannigan's drama club and enjoyed working backstage on lighting, props, and scenery. Later he auditioned for a role and appeared in the production playing the part of a fashion model. He laughed when he described the scenario: "I took off my shirt in the middle of the stage and all the girls went crazy!" He admitted that, although his contribution to the play was not significant, his involvement in drama kept him connected to Mr. Hannigan. The relationship with this teacher became more significant when Joseph spent time with him before and after rehearsals, listening to him discuss the challenges that his older teenage sons and daughter faced that were similar to what Joseph was undergoing in middle school. Mr. Hannigan was also a good listener and became an important confidante for Joseph. Joseph received affirmation from other team teachers who recognized his change of attitude and encouraged him to become even more involved in extracurricular activities. He joined the school district's gospel choir and enjoyed performing with the group. Joseph summarized his middle school experience: "I finally put away my childish side and grew up a bit at that point."

Family Challenges and Transition to High School

A significant historical event had a serious impact on Joseph's life toward the end of his middle school years. The attack on the World Trade Center on September 11, 2001, had ramifications for Joseph's father and his immigration status. When Mr. Ideye began scheduling appointments for meetings with the government immigration office, Joseph began asking questions and eventually learned of important details of his parents' early years as a couple. Serious conversations with his father shed light on the conflict occurring.

Joseph learned that his mother had been involved in drugs early in the marriage. As her addiction became more serious, she became associated with loan sharks and owed them a substantial sum of money. In his attempt to protect his wife, Mr. Ideye questioned the loan sharks as to what he had to do to pay off her debts. He agreed to sell their drugs. When he was caught for drug running, he was incarcerated and charged with a felony. Under immigration law, with a felony charge on his record, he was not able to apply for citizenship or receive a green card. Since that time, he had been waiting for the law to change or to discover a loophole to acquire citizenship. As a result, he struggled to find employment and accepted menial positions in dry cleaning establishments to provide for his son.

Joseph was determined to support his dad. With his father legally restricted from airline travel, Joseph flew to the South in the summer to acquire documents his father would need to prove that he had entered the country legally on his student visa. He spent several weeks reconnecting with his extended family as he pursued several visits to the Office of Vital Statistics and Records in order to obtain official copies of his parents' birth certificates and marriage license and other documents that would be needed in his father's court case. Immigration officials were questioning whether or not Mr. Ideye had legally entered the country because no verification of the visa existed. Before leaving for his trip, Joseph had hopes of reconnecting with his mother; however, upon arrival, he discovered that she had been incarcerated.

When these serious issues began to unfold for Mr. Ideye, Joseph needed to learn all he could to better understand his father's circumstances. That eventful year was a time for serious reflection and soul searching. He explained:

> My ninth-grade year was a year of learning my family's history and attempting to understand where things stood for my father at that time. I had become aware of my father's troubles and I realized I needed to decide what I would do with my life.

He gained important insights in conversations with his father when he was able to question him about his mother and his parents' early years of marriage. He explained:

> Technically, what he should have done was apply for citizenship immediately after they were married. When I asked him why they had not done that, his response was, "Well, at the time, we were young, and we didn't think anything was going to happen. We were married and in love. There was no rush." Then when the felony charge happened, that just messed everything up and prevented him from ever being able to apply for [citizenship]. So he simply tried to make the best out of his situation.

Joseph admired his father and appreciated how hard he worked. He explained, "He definitely tried hard as a father and definitely did the best he could." He continued, "Although we weren't always financially stable, he always would do whatever it took to make sure that I had everything I needed, food to eat, clothes to wear, and a place to live." Joseph admired his father's internal strength and his calm approach to problem solving: "He always tried to see if he could take different routes. At one point he started taking computer classes in hopes of maybe working at a computer firm as a technician or as a consultant." He described his father's optimism: "He may have been frustrated with his immigration status preventing him from moving ahead, but he just kept saying, 'Just pray that this will work out or somehow the law will change.'"

While the challenge of Mr. Ideye's immigration status was evolving, Joseph began his freshman year in a large urban high school of 2,500 students. That summer he delivered newspapers and worked on the landscaping team of a local church in order to help out his father with expenses. Aware of the materialism associated with teenage social status, he saved to buy his own clothes. He explained, "It was that period when your friends were concerned with who was wearing what . . . Timberland boots and Jordans, nice clothes, and all that stuff." During this time, he also saw his peer group splintering into "the ghetto kids," "the prep kids wearing Abercrombie & Fitch," "the Goths," and "the Spanish and Jamaican groups." In the beginning, he stuck to his friends from middle school; however, eventually they agreed they were not compatible and moved on to establish different friendships. He reflected on that year as a year of discovery in that he started to learn what his real strengths were beyond the classroom. He continued his involvement in his church youth group and sang in the church choir. He participated in the high school chorus and performed with the gospel choir. He was elected to the student council and was on the junior varsity football team. With increased involvement in extracurricular activities, his grades improved and he maintained honor roll status.

Although life at school was improving, Joseph's situation at home remained tense. His father's challenges with the immigration office continued, and discussions as to whether or not he would be deported back to Nigeria were occurring. To cope, Joseph kept busy. He developed a second coping mechanism. He explained: "I was dealing with a lot outside of school. I learned to keep my two lives separate. I kept home at home and school at school."

Tenth Grade: A Critical Year With Sara Coleman

When Joseph arrived in Sara Coleman's mathematics class sophomore year, he recognized that this new teacher had a rather unconventional approach to teaching and connected with her from the start. He described her classroom to me:

> She had a lot of kids who were very outspoken. They had their own minds, and some days it was difficult for her to teach a lesson because she was having to compete with them. She turned to me. She wanted me to help control that behavior, so at first, we started with me leading groups. I'd say, "Okay, guys, how are we going to solve this?" Eventually, I worked with her on developing different projects for the class. She enjoyed trying different ways to have us learn the content—group projects and other creative methods.
>
> She always tried to make learning math fun. Problems started out with "Joseph eats 30 chicken nuggets." She was also one of those teachers who would be there to offer afterschool help and projects to help us boost our grades. She let people know from the beginning, "I'm open if you need to talk, if you need help."

Ms. Coleman recognized Joseph's leadership talent and worked to nurture it. He described a number of influential high school teachers who invested time and energy in supporting him; however, he explained that Sara Coleman was the one teacher who said to him, "Okay, you're a leader. How will you plug yourself into other people?" From then on, he went on to lead a variety of groups during the remainder of his high school career.

Joseph had the good fortune of having Sara and her husband move into his neighborhood. The newly married couple purchased a house across the street from Joseph's apartment building. The home was in need of serious renovation, and Sara's father, a contractor, was taking on the project. When she discovered who her new neighbor was, her father hired Joseph to join him and Sara's husband and brothers to work on rebuilding the house. Joseph enjoyed working with the men in Sara's family, and he also had the opportunity to interact with his teacher in a comfortable context.

Sara had learned of Mr. Ideye's situation and questioned Joseph about progress with the immigration case. As they worked on the house, he had the opportunity to share his father's experience and provide updates. By that time, Mr. Ideye had acquired a lawyer to represent him, and Joseph remained hopeful. These conversations with his teacher and her family were helpful, as he pointed out, "I needed to be able to talk about it with someone to get rid of some of the pressure." These conversations with supportive adults were important to Joseph's emotional well-being; however, he incorporated a mature approach in coping with his situation. He described the strategy he implemented:

> When I went to school, I focused on things in school. I was obviously overinvolved. It was easier to think about all that I had to do in my classes and the different things I had to take care of with extracurricular activities than to worry about things at home with my dad. It was easier to do that because when you start combining school with home problems, it just gets all messed up. I learned early on to compartmentalize. I saw that I could block out my problems at home and put them aside and focus on what I needed to get done.

He realized that his situation at home was difficult, yet he did not want to be pitied. He shared a philosophical perspective on his situation that was quite mature for a high school teenager. He explained his view of his resilience:

> I've learned through my experiences that when bad things happen you have to learn how to bounce back from them, to simply take the punches as they come and move forward with your life. I didn't want to overfocus on my problems at home because then I'd be letting them define me. I was in high school and starting to think about what I wanted in life. I also did not want anyone feeling sorry for me. I always knew that my situation was bad, but there were obviously other kids going through a lot worse. I knew others who had abusive or neglectful parents, so I realized I could be grateful and move on from there.

Junior and Senior Year in High School

As the family's lawyer prepared for Mr. Ideye's upcoming deportation hearing in court, Joseph maintained a hectic pace in school. Encouraged by Sara Coleman's view of his leadership potential, he increased his involvement in extracurricular activities. He explained:

> That was part of my answer to the situation. I plugged myself into a lot. I spent more time at school than I did at home. School started at 7:30, and I was there until 6:00 every night. When I was really involved in school and keeping busy, I didn't have time to think, "Oh, look at my life."

Joseph played varsity football during his junior and senior years, took on a leadership role in a chapter of the National Society of Black Engineers (NSBE), served on student council, sang in the gospel choir, and performed with the high school's show choir, a competitive vocal ensemble that performed at Disney World. He worked with his music teacher in forming a chamber choir called "Exhibition." In addition, he was elected vice president of his class in his junior year and class president his senior year.

By his sophomore year, he had learned not to associate with strictly one group of students but to maintain healthy relationships with students from the various subcultures of the student body, and this approach to high school life enabled him to lead effectively. He indicated:

> I learned that you have to be willing to integrate and talk to other students in different groups. I learned that it was definitely possible. I didn't realize early on that I had that quality. One thing that got me through is that I was outgoing and not afraid to walk up to people and say, "Hey, how's it going?" or "What's going on?" That helped me with making friends, getting connected, and getting plugged in.

He maintained leadership roles in his church youth group and began a mentoring program called "Sunday Surrender" in which teenagers from his church worked on Sundays with inner city children by teaching lessons, facilitating games, and providing guidance. In his work as president of the NSBE chapter, he started a new program of preprofessional training for his high school peers, facilitating workshops on writing résumés, presenting oneself professionally, and conducting job interviews. He reflected on his junior and senior years as a time of really developing many new skills through leadership opportunities. Although he realized that keeping busy was one way to cope with the problems at home, he described how passionate he was about school:

> I loved a lot of the activities that I got involved with. I liked leading and I liked being a part of different groups. I loved the singing and I loved football, and I liked leading students. Some people may get overwhelmed and burned out, but that never happened because I just enjoyed what I was doing.

Through his involvement in extracurricular activities, Joseph formed relationships with supportive adults. Joseph described how his relationship with his coach was positive and how other faculty members encouraged him. Along with Sara Coleman, Joseph developed an important relationship with his music teacher, Jeremy Marshall, a compassionate man who quietly made a difference. Joseph described:

> We were planning our ensemble's trip for the competition at Disney World. We had to raise funds for the trip. The cost was $900, and I basically had to do this myself; there was nobody to help. I am still convinced to this day that Mr. Marshall covered it. I had done the calculations. I had raised $300. When I asked him, "How much money do I owe?", he answered, "You don't owe anything." I was stunned. He said, "You're fully paid." I believe somehow he intervened and simply didn't say anything. He was definitely a good person.

Challenge for the Ideye Family

Joseph discussed the events of his father's immigration hearing with controlled emotion. He looked back on that day in the courtroom and realized that his father had relied on a lawyer not well-versed in immigration law and therefore not well-prepared to handle the case. When the day arrived for Mr. Ideye to appear in court, Joseph's aunt and uncle accompanied Joseph. Their hope was that the judge would see that Mr. Ideye had a teenage son and would rule against deportation. Since the immigration issue had begun, a transition in judges had taken place, and the second judge was not as familiar with Mr. Ideye's situation as the initial judge appointed to the case. The crux of the case revolved around the question of whether or not he had entered the country legally. The liberal arts college he had attended as an undergraduate had become defunct. Because no school officials were able to verify his student status, his lawyer failed to produce the documentation he needed to substantiate that he had indeed entered the country legally. The judge regretfully had no other options but to decide in favor of deportation. Joseph's memories of that day in court were somber as he explained, "I'll never forget watching them escort my father out of that room in handcuffs."

It took several months for the deportation to be arranged, and Mr. Ideye was incarcerated until the day of his departure. During that time, Joseph visited his father in prison regularly. He did not have his license to drive at that time, so he would get rides to the prison as often as he could. He described that period:

> It was really difficult. The first time I went I just broke down and sobbed. I didn't want to show my emotions because I knew it would only upset my dad. I don't know if it was the surroundings, but whatever it was, it was very difficult to be there and have conversations with him through a Plexiglas window. All through that time my father was trying to remain optimistic. He was stressing, "It's going to be alright, don't worry about it. It seems bad right now, but I can go home to Nigeria and start over." I think he was simply trying to be encouraging to make me feel better.

Joseph was homeless at age 17. His mother, who had been absent throughout his life, was incarcerated, and his father was now being deported. During this difficult period, he lived with his father's girlfriend and waited for the judicial system to pursue custody issues. He was informed that he would hear from his father just hours before his actual departure from the airport. He understood that in deportation cases, family members were provided very limited information because immigration officials wanted to prevent relatives from coming to the airport and causing a disturbance. On the day of the departure, he received the phone call from his father and learned that he had been transported to Logan Airport in Boston where he would depart for Nigeria.

Leaving High School and Transitioning to University Life

During the time of the deportation, Joseph's conversations with Sara Coleman became more important. When spending time on the home renovation, they had opportunities for private chats as they worked. Joseph said, "At that time, I needed to talk about it because I was becoming introverted. I was turning inward because I didn't want people feeling sorry for me. But I was able to talk to her and that was good." He explained that Sara's family members also checked in with him and offered support: "They encouraged me. They'd say, 'We heard what you're going through, and it's good that you're still moving forward; you're still trying.' Stuff like that was very critical to me at that time."

The deportation occurred during his junior year. During this time, Joseph became intensely focused on the college search process. His school's chapter of the National Society for Black Engineers had established a collaborative relationship with a university chapter of NSBE, in which the college students provided mentoring to high school students interested in their field. Meetings took place on the university campus, and through his leadership of the high school NSBE, Joseph had early exposure to the state university. He also established an important relationship through this work. The university chapter had assigned Solomon Okafor, a young Nigerian engineering major and alumnus of Joseph's high school, to serve as a liaison to their chapter. The two quickly became friends.

Joseph became frustrated with his high school guidance counselor, whom he saw as uninformed, as well as inefficient. In his frustration, he decided that it was important that students see and experience what college life is really like rather than simply rely on campus orientation tours provided by colleges and universities. Joseph explained, "I went to my NSBE board and said, 'Let's forget trying to wait for the school. Let's create our own thing to make it happen.'" With Solomon's help, he established a program called "College 101." Students from the high school chapter of NSBE were paired up with NSBE university students for an entire day. They had breakfast, lunch, and dinner with their partners, attended all classes, traveled the campus, studied with their partners, and left with an authentic view of a typical day in the life of an undergraduate. Joseph summarized the reaction of the students: "It was a more authentic experience. It opened their eyes. They saw the academic part of college and not just the parties. They enjoyed it and they appreciated it."

Toward the end of his junior year, Joseph's aunt and uncle succeeded in acquiring temporary custody of him. The court decided it was in his best interests to live with his Nigerian relatives until he was 18, when he would leave for college. By senior year, Joseph was determined to submit all of his college applications for early admission. He discovered that when he needed answers to his application questions, Solomon was someone he could rely on for accurate information and assistance. He described his help:

> I am so grateful for my connection with Solomon. He helped me with a lot of things that my guidance counselor didn't even know. He was informing me of the paperwork that was required. It got to the point where I would actually walk up to my guidance counselor and say, "Okay, you need to send this form and this form, and please make sure they are mailed by this date." I wasn't asking for his advice any more. I was telling him what I needed to make sure I got into college. So it was really great that I had Solomon as a mentor at that time.

As a strong writer, Joseph found that composing his college essays was not overwhelming. Joseph shared them with teachers and Solomon and received helpful editorial feedback. He had no difficulty acquiring strong letters of recommendation from Sara Coleman, other faculty members, and his high school's principal. With a 3.3 grade point average, strong SAT scores, an impressive résumé of extracurricular activities and community service, and praiseworthy letters of reference, he was well prepared to compete for placements in the schools of his choice. He applied to four institutions: a large state university in New England, a large urban university in New England, a smaller college with a Baptist orientation, and a large urban school in the South. He considered various factors in applying to these schools, including proximity to friends and family, size of school, Christian orientation, and program of study.

Joseph realized early in this process that the deciding factor ultimately would be offers of financial aid. He learned of his acceptance to all four institutions by December of his senior year, and then waited to hear from them regarding financial assistance.

The large New England state research university offered Joseph the strongest financial package, and he was delighted to accept it. With that decision in place by early winter, he determined his major. During his senior year, he was enrolled in an allied health class, which he enjoyed and for which he received college credit. Thinking the medical track would be the direction he would take, he decided to major in biology. When he received his acceptance letter to the university, he was informed that he had been selected for a summer bridge program designed to support diverse students from low-income backgrounds with coursework to assist them in their transition to university coursework. Shortly after, he was informed that he had been shifted to a more specialized program known as the Pre-Collegiate Enrichment Program (PCEP) that focused on students pursuing a medical track as undergraduates. The objectives behind this program included helping students make connections with researchers in the medical field in order to be better prepared for medical school. Joseph was delighted to learn that he was one of only 15 students selected for this honor.

He began the program 3 days after his high school graduation. He was enrolled in four rigorous summer classes, including math, English, biology, and chemistry, earning three college credits in math and a modest financial stipend. He referred to the experience as "college boot camp" and described how he was stunned when the program staff appeared on the first day wearing army fatigues! Following 6 weeks of dormitory life, cafeteria food, and serious study, Joseph believed the benefits of the program would provide him with a less stressful beginning when his first fall semester began. He recognized that his familiarity with the large campus and university resources would be an asset, but more importantly, the significant relationships with the other 14 students who had survived the program would become important friendships that would last long after their college graduation.

Joseph's University Years

Joseph enjoyed his first year at the university. He moved into a freshman dormitory and quickly established important new friendships with the young men on his floor while also maintaining his friendships from PCEP. He enjoyed university athletic events and searched for the right extracurricular activities to engage in. He was fortunate to acquire a part-time job with the athletic department in which he helped out with operations at the football stadium and basketball coliseum. He worked between 10 and 15 hours on weekends for additional spending money.

His challenges in adjustment to university life involved being enrolled in large auditorium-sized classes with more than 400 students, with professors lecturing and graduate students serving as teaching assistants. The impersonal nature of these classes was problematic for him: "If you have questions about the class, you take them to a teaching assistant. The professor doesn't even know who you are." During that year he struggled with his biology and chemistry classes and was required to enroll in them again in order to continue with his major. He repeated the courses in the fall of his sophomore year and did not do much better. With that he reconsidered his plan, switched his major to political science, and seriously reflected on how he would repair the damage done to his grade point average. Eventually Joseph grew tired of the social life on campus. His Nigerian family had raised him according to the conservative values of his culture, and he found the weekend parties and drinking to be tiresome. He described his predicament:

> It begins on Thursday nights, and it's all weekend. I tolerated it for a year, but for the most part, I go out to be the chaperone. I make sure my friends don't either end up getting beat up or sleeping on the side of the road by the end of the night. I'm there to make sure they're safe. So many people say to me, "Ohh! You go to such a good school!" And I respond, "Yes, academically, it's a really good school, but socially, it's not where I want to be."

Much of Joseph's university life centered on his involvement in a new church on campus. During his sophomore year, he met with the youth pastor of his home congregation who was interested in beginning a church at the university. He requested help from Joseph, who explained his involvement in the process:

> We spent a lot of time meeting, talking about what we wanted in a church, and what God wanted us to do on campus. We then had to look for a location for services. We spent a lot of time talking with community members and a committee of religious leaders in the campus community. Once we had a space, we had to figure out ways to promote the church and get students to come. I was the person with the contacts so I arranged to have the church represented at the "Welcome to the University" events for incoming students.

Joseph was pleased to report that the new church on campus had acquired a regular venue in one of the most accessible buildings on campus and the congregation had grown to approximately 30 students. He explained that each week he was responsible for organizing rehearsals for the chorus, and smiled as he reported that he was "head of the worship team," which meant that he sang and lead the chorus in Sunday services. He also served on the executive board of the church and worked closely with the youth pastor. He concluded: "This church has played an important role in my life here at the university."

A New Chapter

During his sophomore year, parents of one of Joseph's friends requested a favor of him. They asked him to make a long road trip to deliver their son to his new college. Joseph's friend had withdrawn from a small community college with a miserable academic record following his freshman year. After taking time off from school, he decided to apply to a Christian university in a mid-Atlantic state. Joseph had helped his friend with his application, college essay, and financial aid paperwork and was happy to make the trip. He spent several days visiting the Christian campus and enjoyed what he experienced. During spring break from the university, he made a second trip to explore the school further. He spent time attending classes, met students, and had meetings with professors in the political science department. He was pleased with the less competitive and more collaborative culture of the school. He was impressed with the academic program, as well as the school's atmosphere, and decided to apply for admission. At the time of my final interview with Joseph, he had received his acceptance letter and was awaiting news of financial aid. He described the atmosphere of the school:

> The community has a contract with the school. There are no bars in town and no party spots to tempt students off campus. The school maintains a curfew, but there is little to do in the community so that works out well. They stress taking the clean and narrow path and finding alternate ways of having fun.

He corresponded with his father and found he was supportive of Joseph's plan. His father wrote: "I know that whatever you do, you will follow your religious values." Although Joseph knew it would be difficult to leave so many good friends in New England, he was excited about transferring to the new school. "I'm looking at this as a new start and an opportunity to meet new people." Joseph concluded, "I think it will be a better match for my Christian lifestyle. I am thinking I can get the Christian foundation that I really want from the school as an undergrad before I decide on graduate school or law school."

Toward the end of our interviews, Joseph informed me that his mother was out of prison and was pursuing drug rehabilitation. He prayed that her life would improve. He reflected on the important relationship he shared with his father: "We have the closest relationship. Growing up, he was all I had, and I was all he had. We grew up together. That special bond remains very strong." He was happy to report that his father had moved on with his life in Nigeria. He was working hard to begin a new dry cleaning business in his community. With the experience and expertise he had acquired in the United States, he was well prepared to provide a service that was nonexistent where he was currently living. Joseph was also pleased to report that religion had become an important part of his father's new life. He had joined a church and was working to support it in a variety of ways. He had been in touch with Joseph to see if he might help him acquire used copies of Bibles that could be used by his religious community.

Our final conversation took place in a coffee shop on a blustery winter day. As we enjoyed tall mugs of hot chocolate, Joseph shared his thoughts on what he believed enables young people to overcome life's adversities. He offered the following:

> One thing that I know for sure is having some kind of foundation, whether it's a religious foundation or a family foundation, somewhere where you can get support. It doesn't have to be your family. It can be teachers or other people in your life. I definitely utilized that a lot, particularly my teachers. . . . I think the other issue that is more important is being able to just let things hit you without letting them knock you down. I went through a lot, but obviously there are people who have gone through worse. I know the one thing that I have always told myself is, "Okay, well that happened, but there is nothing that you can do to change it, so just move on and try to make the best of this bad situation." If you let the adversity in your life take over, you cut yourself off from so many opportunities that you could enjoy if you just persevere. I'm not saying ignore it. I'm not saying lock it up inside of you. I'm saying let it go and just move on. I see a lot of self-help books today that deal with overcoming your adversity, but they don't teach you how to grow from it. You have to use it and help others. It's not just about you all the time. You have to be able to incorporate your struggles to help other people. That's how I try to look at everything.

Epilogue

Joseph enjoyed his years as a student at the Christian university, earning his bachelor's and master's degrees in political science. While pursuing his graduate degree, he was employed as a case manager in a firm providing long-term healthcare planning. He currently lives in the upper Midwest and is enjoying his work as an environmental technician for a company associated with maintaining occupational safety standards. He hopes to visit his father in Nigeria in the near future.

CHAPTER 2

KEITH

I waited in the lobby of my hotel and watched guests dressed in ski parkas and hats attaching skis and ski poles to the roofs of their cars. With the sun shining after a winter snowfall, they were bound to enjoy a great day on the nearby slopes. A sporty SUV pulled up to the hotel entrance, and the driver smiled at me and waved. I climbed in and was delighted to meet Keith Walton. We shared pleasantries, discussing the newly fallen snow and my travels to the area the day before. I had driven from my home to this university community in the scenic Appalachian Mountains and had enjoyed a relaxing evening in a cozy and rustic inn. He questioned me about my first night at the inn, wanting to be sure I was comfortable and the nearby restaurant was enjoyable. Keith was employed at the university, and we had earlier agreed to conduct the interviews on campus. As we drove to the university, he provided commentary about the local area and seemed delighted to share what he knew of the history of this bucolic mountain setting.

That morning Keith was dressed in causal khakis, a tweed sports jacket, and a buttoned-down shirt—the look of a young academic. With sandy blonde hair and an athletic physique, he was both energetic and outgoing and seemed happy to have me as a guest. Keith was a faculty member in the communications department and director of the debate program on campus. When we arrived at his office, he introduced me to several students and his wife, Margaret, who was also employed at the college. She graciously invited me to join them for a family dinner at home during my stay, and I accepted. We got situated in Keith's office for our first interview, and I soon realized that Keith would be easy to work with, as the conversation flowed naturally and he was eager to share his work at the university. I also realized that we had made a mistake in holding the conversation in his office. Interruptions from students knocking on the door forced us to stop several times. When this occurred, Keith and I agreed that we needed to conduct our work together elsewhere on campus, so we booked a conference room at the university's library for the remainder of the week and found the privacy we needed.

Keith's story is that of a talented young man from a culture of poverty. He was misunderstood and often neglected, seriously bullied in school, and confronted family dysfunction throughout his adolescence before reaching the professional success he enjoyed at the university.

Keith's Childhood

Keith was the only son and the youngest child in a family of three. As a toddler, he enjoyed a warm relationship with his two older sisters, Cathy and Desiree. Following a short courtship, Keith's parents were married in what he described as a "bit of a shotgun wedding" when they were 18. Both had dropped out of high school. They settled in an oil mining community in California, lived near extended family members, and remained in the same city all of their lives. Mr. Walton was employed as an oil rig operator—a "roughneck"—in the oil fields, and his wife remained home to care for her three children. Keith pointed out that when the oil industry was healthy, his dad often worked double shifts: "He'd be working 16 hours a day to put food on the table." Keith described his parents' marriage as stable. "They never had any marital problems. Their only problem was dealing with not having enough money to pay the bills." He explained that he lived in the same city from the time he was 5 years old until his sophomore year in high school except for a "a 3-month period when we moved 17 times." The transitions from multiple neighborhoods resulted from difficult financial challenges for the family. He explained:

> We'd move into a house, and either we couldn't pay the bills, or it wasn't a safe neighborhood, or my mom would just not get a good feeling about where we lived. She'd see a mouse, so we'd move the next weekend. I remember one situation when my dad was out of work again, and I was saying that I wanted to stay in what was a relatively nice neighborhood. I couldn't understand why we had to move back to another bad neighborhood. My mom finally explained, "We don't have the money to stay here." That was probably the first time I recognized it consciously. There was something called money that meant something, and different people could have different experiences because of that.

Keith described his parents' response to their situation: "My parents are very proud people. They are products of their families, who grew up during the Great Depression. They didn't ask for much, and they never lived beyond their means." He continued, "They never signed up for unemployment benefits or welfare. They were just too prideful." He reflected, "I was on free lunch when I was in kindergarten and first grade, so we must have been below the poverty line to qualify." He described his response to his family's situation:

> I realized that there were kids around me who had distinctly more. Peter was a kid who lived about five blocks over, and I'd go to his house and I distinctly remember thinking he had more. But it didn't make me say, "Bring your cool stuff over to my house." . . . I remember getting these Stars Wars hand-me-downs from my cousins when they grew out of them, and I was like, "Wow! I don't know what this is, but it's cool." . . . I was the kid that you could take to the junk store, and I'd find something, and it would be so cool to me. If the G. I. Joe didn't have an arm, that was okay. He had lost his arm in the war [laughs]. I was just that kind of kid. I'd find a stick, and we'd play stickball for hours, or we'd entertain ourselves digging a hole.

His memories of his early years in school were quite vivid. With a mom who stayed home to care for her children, Keith had no experience with preschool programs, and he spent several days in tears at the beginning of his kindergarten transition. Teachers soon recognized that he was rather precocious:

> When I first got to kindergarten, I was quite verbal. About a month in, when we started learning our letters, they realized I was actually really smart. With math, they would have me do 9 times 1, times 2, times 3 . . . they were called CAT tests. I was the top kid in the class because I got to 9. There were three of us who would get pulled aside to work on things. I realize now it was the early version of gifted classes. We never left the room; we went to the other side of the room. By the time I started first grade, I could do all 12, so they kept advancing me in math. I remember being in first and second grade, and my older sisters had me doing their homework, so I was already doing fractions.

Keith's reflections of his elementary school years focused on particular teachers. He remembered his first-grade teacher, a woman he viewed as "not warm" who "pulled the yellow card." He explained, "I was one of those kids who prided myself on not getting in trouble. She pulled the yellow card! Green card means you've been good. Yellow means you've been warned, and red means you're going to see the principal." His second-grade teacher was one of the warmest and most engaging. He smiled as he explained how he responded to her: "She had a star system for rewards. My friend Eric and I were the only two who competed for stars. If you sat with your hands crossed at your seat and were quiet after recess, you'd get a star." Fourth grade involved a difficult transition to an overcrowded hybrid fourth- and fifth-grade class where the work was not challenging. He encountered his first male teacher in fifth grade, who was influential. He said, "Dr. Dow was an older gentleman and very nice. One of the things I remember about him was that he'd brush his teeth in the morning, at lunch, and right before we left school, and I thought that was fascinating." He described Dr. Dow's approach to teaching math:

> He'd have these activities that we'd do in math that were fun. He'd say, "You're going to McDonald's. Here's the menu. You're going to buy these items. How much will it cost? And don't forget to add the tax." I always got those right. As a fifth grader, who didn't want to go to McDonald's?!

Keith saw Dr. Dow as a "grandfather" figure: "Not just manly, but he'd present a message that said, 'Stand back, but know that I care about you and we're going to learn.' I did well with that approach." He described his fondest memory of his year with Dr. Dow:

> I missed a day, and one of my friends reported that Dr. Dow had a big lesson in math that particular day, and he announced that I was the best math student that he'd ever had and he was disappointed that I wasn't there. Being told that by my friend, I knew that he didn't make that story up. That comment was so important to me.

Support from teachers like Dr. Dow was critical to Keith at a time when he was beginning to understand his family's challenging circumstances. His sixth-grade teacher was also influential:

> My literacy experience early on was meager. I think we had maybe four or five books that had been given to my family. I don't remember ever seeing my older sisters reading at home. I don't remember my parents ever reading to me as a child. I don't think that I actually read my first complete book until I was in sixth grade. It was *The Island on Bird Street* by Uri Orlev, and my teacher Mr. Eastman suggested that I read this book because I was in the accelerated program. . . . My family was very poor. Today my wife and I will ask our kids, "What do you want for dinner?" That was not the question my sisters and I heard. We got what we had for supper. We got our share, and we didn't get anything else. . . . So the feeling of extreme poverty that the boy in the novel was experiencing was very parallel to my life. I don't know if my teacher was wise enough to recognize that that was my life and that I'd identify with the character, or if he just thought that it was a good book and I'd enjoy it. I remember reading that book at home, and I remember my mom asking, "What are you doing?" And I said, "I'm reading a book." And she said, "That's great!"

Keith faced difficult challenges in middle school. With so many family moves, he was forced to switch schools several times during the academic year, and establishing friendships in each new school was hard. He discovered quickly in each setting that he did not fit in with the majority of students, and he encountered severe bullying. He explained how he had several strikes against him during these tough transitions:

In sixth grade, I arrived at a new school in October. The school population consisted of a majority of Latino and Black students. I was placed in an overcrowded classroom of 35 kids, another hybrid class. I took a seat in the back corner away from everyone. One challenge I had was that in sixth grade, I stayed at 5'1", and all the other guys grew to giant size in my mind. My birthday is in late September so I started kindergarten when I was 4. I was younger than everyone else, smaller, and they were not my friends. I was severely bullied. . . . The bullies I faced were Hispanic boys. I remember feeling like my life was in danger many times.

Keith rode his bike to school early in order to strategically lock his bicycle close to his classroom door, knowing that he would be able to get out of the building at the end of the day. He said, "Every afternoon, I was able to run, get my bike, and I'd see them [the bullies] running after me. Recess was hell." He took note of the demographics of the school and theorized as to why he was experiencing the bullying. He pointed out he was accelerated in math and involved in gifted and talented education (GATE) classes. He explained,

I'd look around and think, "How many White kids are here?" The White kids were always in the GATE classes with me, so I knew there had to be about 20 or 30. I didn't have many friends, and the few friends I had certainly were not going to protect me or defend me in any shape or form.

He struggled to understand the reason for the bullying he experienced. He said, "I think the resentment was due to the fact that I left my classroom for GATE and I left for Math Bowl team competitions. But I never heard them say, 'Hey, smart kid.' It was always, 'Hey, honky.'"

His parents sensed that he was having trouble and was not happy. He was timid about reporting the bullying because he believed his father would have responded with, "Punch them in the nose when they come near you, even if you have to get beat up. If you punch them hard enough, they'll leave you alone." During this difficult time, he recognized that his father was preoccupied with his own worries:

My father was laid off from work. There was a recession, but the oil company heard a rumor that a lot of the oil workers were wanting to unionize, so the company used the opportunity to exercise some power. My father lost his job for a 6-month period. We very shortly ran out of money. We were having to eat off the gifts of others, not benefits from the government, but luckily people were nice. During that period of time, we literally ate beans and cornbread for every meal. The corn mix was a gift from somebody. I can't remember who it was. The beans were cheap and had the protein that my mother thought we needed, and that's what we ate. It was a difficult period, and I think back on it every so often. My wife, Margaret, loves beans and cornbread, coincidentally, and so whenever she makes it, I am taken back to that moment in my life, and I'm reminded of how little we had at different times. Those are the nights I find myself reflecting on all the things we now own, and I go through that existential crisis of saying, "Why do we need all of this stuff?"

At the end of sixth grade, Keith's family was forced to move again, and his parents gave him a choice about which school he would attend. He explained:

I ended up in a district that encompassed a suburb of fairly wealthy White kids. There were some minority kids there, too, but the really rich kids all wore surfer-skate brands of clothing. I wore sweatpants and sweatshirts that were too big. Needless to say, I didn't fit in. I went from being the only White kid to being the only poor White kid. In this school, you were either a White rich kid from an oil family or you were either a very poor Hispanic or Black kid. That was the demographic of the school. I was not a rich White kid, and I wasn't a student of color, which meant I fit in with nobody.

To add to his problems, he was not scheduled into accelerated classes. Instead he was placed in general education classes. He described this point as "the moment in time when I made the conscious decision not to care about grades and education." He said, "This was an incredibly difficult period. I took an 'I don't care attitude' and found many reasons to stay home."

This period was also when Keith was resentful of his father. He explained it as his pubescent response when he clearly communicated that he was not interested in being around his father. He understood that it was a normal process for an adolescent male to distance himself from his father to become his own person; however, he regretted having been so rude to his dad. He continued, "In my mind, I blamed him for that 3-month period when we moved so often. I blamed him for making me live in this poor area and dropping me off to school with all the rich kids." He reflected, "All that social stuff I was getting from the other kids. I was projecting onto him."

Lacking the skills to negotiate a large school bureaucracy, Keith's parents did not advocate for their son in school. Instead, his father encouraged him to begin playing football. To appease his father, he went along with the plan. He explained, "My father was a varsity player in his freshman year of high school. He was a star defensive back." His father talked with a number of coaches in the various leagues throughout the area. Keith smiled as he said,

> I ended up on a team with kids from a lot of tough neighborhoods. I was one of two White kids on the team. Thankfully, I was not the goofiest nor the least athletic of the two White kids, but I was distinctly overweight. I put on a lot of weight in seventh and eighth grade. I was 180 pounds in eighth grade. Coaches would say, "You need to be offensive line because of your size." My response was, "But I'm fat and not strong!"

During this period, Keith's parents focused their attention on his older sister Desiree. He described how his parents were concerned about the young men she was dating and the crowd of teenagers she befriended. She was associated with gangs and would often be involved in fights at school. Keith pointed out, "all the girls were afraid of her, and she was attractive so the gangster guys wanted to be friends with her." He explained, "She ran away from home at least three times that I remember. She was often in trouble with the law, whether it was shoplifting or drugs." He reflected on one particular dramatic evening:

> I remember one time when she'd been missing. I was in the car with my parents searching all over for her, and my parents

found out she was at this pool parlor in town that was known for serving alcohol to underage minors. When we got there, I remember her running and my dad chasing after her and finally tackling her to the ground. There was this dramatic scene when the police arrived to say that my dad had attacked her. They had my dad in handcuffs and were going to press charges. Eventually she was placed in a counseling program and moved into a halfway house for a month.

He described the family's response. He said, "I distinctly remember the pain and anguish that it caused my mom and dad and the feeling of hopelessness they had." He also reflected on how his sister's experience influenced him: "Being the observant kid that I was, that was the reason I just couldn't do that to my parents. I learned a lot from Desiree's mistakes, and I was able to stay away from that stuff."

Desiree's experiences in school also had an effect on her younger brother. She was a high school senior when Keith began his freshman year. Although he weighed 180 pounds and had grown a foot taller by the time he arrived in high school, he maintained that his older sister's affiliation with gang members had an impact. With her established reputation for fights in school and being an attractive and influential leader amongst her peers, Keith explained, "I'm sure all the guys wanted to be friends with her, so they never bothered me."

Keith's High School Experience

During his transition from middle school to high school, Keith made an important decision that helped to shape his high school experience. He attended a large high school, which he described: "The school was surrounded by chain-linked fences with barbwire to keep people out. Kids brought guns to school every day. Drugs and gangs were a big issue." He explained, "For that period of time from sixth grade to right before high school, nobody cared who I was. When I got to high school, I was empowered by theatre." He saw theatre as an "opportunity to speak and be listened to." When he decided to become involved in the theatre group, there were few male actors for parts needed in the scheduled productions. The drama coach, Mr. Warner, encouraged him to audition for the spring production. Keith described his initial experience:

> We did *Julius Caesar*, and because we had so few men, we reversed the roles so Julius Caesar and Cassius, and everybody else became a female biker gang. I played Calpurnia. I played Caesar's boyfriend or husband. I doubt that I was any good, but it felt wonderful. My family was in the audience that first night. Just that feeling of succeeding, I loved it.

From freshman year through his junior year, Keith remained involved in theatre and enjoyed competing in annual regional Shakespearean festivals, playing the role of one of the mechanicals in *A Midsummer Night's Dream* and the ghost of Hamlet's father in *Hamlet*. He enjoyed the camaraderie of the kids in theatre. "All these artsy, creative kids, probably classic underachievers because I doubt that any of them really excelled in academics, but they were all smart and interesting." He mentioned, "By freshman year, I was much taller, quite thin, cute, and one of the few boys in theatre, so I got to experience some of my first interactions with girls, all these free-spirited types, and that was fun." He elaborated on the importance of the theatre experience:

> So there I was, this kid who has never read and never been interested in Shakespeare, and the whole world was opened up to me. Let's not kid ourselves. Shakespeare is not easy to read nor easy to say, but Mr. Warner was such a good developer of character, and I found these people fascinating. Theatre . . . felt nice and warm and invited. I guess in ninth and tenth grade, I'd come out of that period where I was reclusive and antisocial. I had all of these difficult experiences that were bottled up, and theatre was my safe place to go to. It was probably the first time I got to be creative and the only time I ever felt people wanted to listen to what I had to say. I felt like I had something to say—even if they weren't my words, they were someone else's words. I certainly wasn't Calpurnia or the others characters I was playing. I got to be somebody else, and that was wonderful. I guess theatre allowed me to enjoy some notion of what self-esteem was all about.

Along with finding his creative outlet in theatre, Keith discovered another outlet for his voice. In selecting an elective course as a freshman, he chose forensics. He chuckled as he described his introduction to debate:

> I found debate coincidentally. It was called forensics. I thought it was detective work, but it meant speech and development. This was before the *Crime Scene Investigation* television show [laughs]. I was enjoying theatre, and I thought I could either act or I could be a detective. I thought being a cop might be a good opportunity. Lo and behold, I showed up on the first day of class, and it was not forensics! That was an interesting experience. I didn't think I was going to like it, but I absolutely loved it and stayed with it all 4 years. Thankfully, in spite of not being a great high school, we had a great debate team with a coach who had been around a long time.

Keith played high school football during his freshman and sophomore years. He described his teammates as "a group of mean, crass young men who objectified women sexually and boasted about passing along girls," and he was uncomfortable dealing with this mentality. He also found that football was predictable. He said, "My job was to block the defensive end most plays. I did my job but it was so monotonous." Another teammate who was also in the theatre group faced a similar situation. He explained, "Rob hated football, too, but he had the same father situation where his father was a football player, so he was also under a lot of pressure to play." He struggled with his decision to quit football, agonizing over how his father would respond to the news. When he explained to his father that he was much more interested in devoting his energy to drama and debate, he was stunned when his father responded with, "Well, you know what? That's alright with me because you're talented in many ways. Everything you do, you do well. If that's what you want to do, then I'll be there." Keith was hugely relieved and appreciated that his father fulfilled his promise, "He came to every play and every debate tournament."

The debate coach, Mr. Beale, was a seasoned coach who had a long history of success with teams that qualified in the National Debate Tournament. The team was responsible for the Lincoln-Douglas debate, which was a one-on-one debate, as well as policy debate, which involved two-on-two debates. Keith was paired with Marcus, an African American student who became a good friend. He said, "Marcus and I started to debate together. We worked well together and met instant success." Shortly after he established the partnership with Marcus, he reflected on his theatre experience and did some soul searching:

> Theatre was interesting and fun, and I had good friends there, but I knew I wasn't going to be a playwright. I knew I wasn't going to be an actor. I knew I wasn't going to be a director, and in debate, I was able to create my own. In the research of the arguments, in the construction of the arguments, you really get to create information and knowledge. I got to experience that, and it was wonderful. In theatre, I had something to say and I felt important, but here I was now on a successful debate team. I was writing up arguments, and I thought that was wonderful. That tipped me over and made me decide debate is really what I wanted to do.

His introduction to debate also involved an introduction to an inspirational teacher. As a freshman, Keith had Mr. Beale for an Honors English class, as well as forensics. He saw Mr. Beale as an incredibly intelligent man who was well-versed in multiple disciplines. He was immediately impressed with this teacher. He described his initial days in Mr. Beale's classroom:

> I had his Honors English class, and one of the first things we did was dissect two songs, [one] by Bob Dylan, "Just Upon Us" [sic], and [one] by Counting Crows, "Mr. Jones." "Mr. Jones" was a song that had just been released, a new song that I liked, and we broke it down from a literary perspective. Then we did the same with "Just Upon Us." What he was trying to do was to take his generation's song and our generation's song and meld them together to build a commonality with us. I thought he was fantastic. I saw him twice a day and it was great.

Keith enjoyed preparing for his first debate tournament with Mr. Beale. He had a positive experience in the debate and felt good about it, yet he learned another important lesson:

> I did the Lincoln-Douglas debate, which was the one-on-one, and I won my hour round, so I technically finished with a bronze medal in the tournament. I thought "Wow! This is great." One of the interesting experiences I had that day was another lesson I learned. My father and other men in my family don't wear suits and ties. They don't have dress clothes. I was told to wear dress clothes. So I put on my eighth-grade dance clothes, and my grandfather had a rope tie with a big ole' medallion. That's what I had on, and all these other kids were decked out in three-piece suits, the whole nine yards. I remember thinking, "Okay, here I am again, and I don't fit in again."

In his second tournament, he and Marcus competed as a duo in a policy debate and brought home a gold medal. "That feeling of success, having my father in attendance, bringing home medals and trophies . . . It was wonderful. These early experiences with success helped to grow my passion for debate. This was really the turning point in shifting from theatre and having debate take the prominent role in my life." Early in his sophomore year, Keith and his teammates traveled to an Ivy League university for a tournament, which was a crystalizing experience for him:

> Seeing that campus with all the coffee houses and the hole-in-the-wall pizza shops, the artistic kids, the bookstores and all the libraries, it really just epitomized the most creative and scientifically advanced place in the world to me. It was just fascinating. But the one thing that really amazed me was the free speech area. Somebody was out there spouting something, and the crowd was cheering him on. I think the message was anti-war. I remember Marcus and I sitting there and just observing all of this, and we were like, "Wow, I guess this is what it's all about." We hadn't had that experience in high school, and the closest thing to it was our debate team.

At that particular debate tournament, Keith realized the seriousness of the competition his team faced. He indicated, "We were coming from a high school where we held fund raisers to pay for the team to be involved in these tournaments. We were competing against wealthy magnet schools with tons of money budgeted to send teams. We were coming from nowhere and were being challenged by those with so much." He saw that experience as "real catalyst" that motivated him to work:

> Marcus and I decided, "Okay, we're going to do this!" We would spend hours every day doing research, organizing, and practicing. We finished second in the junior varsity division in one tournament and then came back to the next one and beat, in the first round, the team that had won the varsity division at the last tournament. This was the moment when we knew we had arrived. It was such a great moment, such a great feeling.

Keith maintained that school had always been easy for him and he had never learned to work hard. He indicated, "I never did homework. I was in the GATE programs, and they were easy." He reflected on his dark middle school years: "When math got difficult in seventh grade, I responded by just taking an 'it's really not important' attitude and created that cover of 'nobody expects much from me.'... With debate, I realized you cannot succeed if you don't work." He described how the rigor of debate made a difference for him:

> Debate rounds are about 2 hours long. Intense conversation between four people, 8- or 9-minute speeches, 6-minute rebuttal, cross examination, and preparation. To succeed, you have to be able to focus for long periods of time. You don't just have one debate; you have four debates per day. That's 8 hours, and in between you're working on things that you know didn't work the last time that have to be changed. So these were long days, 10 or 12 hours, [which] required intense mental dexterity. This is where I learned that not everything came easy. Debate pushed me and taught me the mental dexterity to achieve. The debate experience was the first time I was really intellectually challenged. That experience was so vital for my life.

He reflected on how the influence of debate extended beyond high school:

> I owe a debt of gratitude to Mr. Beale for everything that he did for me and because of what debate has done for me in my life. It's helped me to become a much better person.... Debate

> is the art of critical thinking and problem solving. It made me question things I never would have questioned. It made me see things from all different perspectives and sides. It helped me to meet people from where they were coming from. It has helped me develop the ability to be truthful with myself, to be able to honestly look at my behavior, my beliefs, my life, and say, "This is right. This is wrong. This is why I honestly do this."

Keith's academic program of study changed after his sophomore year. He was enrolled in more honors classes, and by his senior year, he took Advanced Placement courses. Math Bowl and debate were his extracurricular activities. Throughout middle and high school, much of his time was spent working part-time jobs. When he was 12, he was paid under the table to work as a janitor in a bowling alley. Later, he worked at a liquor store stocking shelves, and eventually, he worked in a sandwich shop making and delivering sandwiches. With his money, he purchased a "hand-me-down Chevy pickup truck" and had to pay for insurance and gas. Conversations about his plans for after high school did not happen until halfway through his senior year. He realized that he would be the first in his family to walk across the graduation stage, as his parents and his sisters had all dropped out of high school and eventually earned their GEDs. As he was enjoying his debate experience, he began discussing colleges with good debate teams, and his mother would respond with a question: "Are you sure you want to go to college?" He was certain his father was waiting for him to ask about introducing him to the people he worked for, so he, too, could get a job in the oil fields after high school. Eventually his parents asked, "Are you going to work in a sandwich shop your whole life? What are you planning to do?"

He acknowledged his high school transcripts reflected an inconsistent record. He had been enrolled in a variety of college prep, honors, and Advanced Placement courses, was graduating with a grade point average of 2.90, and was ranked 81st in a class of 581, a clear indication that high academic achievement was not a priority for many of the school's seniors. His girlfriend at that time was planning on taking the SATs, and he decided to join her.

The Undergraduate and Graduate School Years

Upon graduation from high school at age 17, Keith moved into an apartment in the city with an older cousin who worked with him in the sandwich shop. Keith qualified for federal educational Pell grants and enrolled in a local community college. He accepted a job washing dishes in a family-style restaurant, working nights and weekends, and managed to complete a year's worth of required general education courses, earning a grade of A in every course but one. He joined the college's debate team and was soon recruited for debate by three different universities. When two of the schools were unable to offer him the funding he needed, he called Dan Truman, the director of the debate program at the third school. Dan had observed Keith competing in the junior college national tournament, winning gold medals in several categories, and receiving a prestigious award from his peers. When Keith inquired about a place for him on the debate team, Dan responded, "Absolutely! I'll have money for you tomorrow, and you can live at my house until you find housing."

Dan met Keith at the airport when he arrived. Situated in a rural southeastern state, the mid-sized regional university had a rich tradition of success in debate. Dan purposefully drove through the backwoods roads to the school in order to have more time for conversation in the car with his new recruit. Keith smiled as he explained, "I was thinking 'What have I done? How quickly can I get back on a plane to go home'?" The following day, Dan helped him with the university's bureaucratic paperwork and provided him a tour of the campus. Keith described his response to his new environment:

> As I walked around campus, I thought, "Okay, it's a real school. It has a library, I can do this. I met some of the debate team members, and I thought, "Okay, I can get along with these people." I got homesick pretty quick, but I worked through it fast. Within a few weeks, I was fine.

In his first year of college, he indicated that he enjoyed "getting away from family and all the confines that are placed around your identity from being raised in an area." He enjoyed his friendship with an openly gay student with whom he shared an apartment. He explored a variety of churches, "trying to get a better sense of myself and these notions of religion, what is God, and questions about bigger issues than just me in this world." In his role as debate coach, Dan Truman was influential. He also served as an advisor to a Greek fraternity on campus. Keith joined two fellow debate team members and pledged the fraternity when he understood the group was grounded in Christian values. He enjoyed the social functions, but emphasized that he enjoyed the personal development readings and discussion sessions that were part of the fraternity's culture even more.

Keith was grateful for the full tuition scholarship he received. The university waived his out-of-state tuition and paid his in-state tuition. A student loan covered his books and housing. To pay for food and other small expenses, he washed dishes at a local restaurant and later worked as a night auditor for a hotel, which he maintained "nearly destroyed" him. He said, "I was up from 11 to 7 and then in class from 9 to 4, but I always had to work. I had to eat." He explained:

> I lived off the money that I made, which was about $60 a week. When there were sales, I would buy crates of Ramen noodles and stock up on canned soups. But it was just the way it was. When we went to debate tournaments, they gave us meal money. I ate best when we were traveling to tournaments.

Keith highlighted that the camaraderie of the debate team members was most important to him during his 3 years at the university, and the debate experience kept him there.

During his second day on campus, he met Margaret in the debate program office. He described himself "being awestruck." He investigated and learned that she was "still off and on with her old boyfriend," but later when he had the chance to spend time with her on the debate team bus, the two really "hit it off"—"She was smart, she was beautiful, she was interesting. There was fire and passion, and there was vulnerability and sensitivity. She encompassed this whole range of emotions that I had always felt but could never express." They dated for a year and a half, and they were married in December during the holiday break between semesters. Dan Truman served as best man and arranged to have the intimate ceremony in his Baptist church followed by a reception for 12 people at the only place in town that served liquor. The following morning, Keith drove his new bride to California to meet his parents. He had shared the important news with his parents over the phone earlier. He chuckled as he reported, "By the time we arrived, they had redecorated the guest bedroom in this honeymoon motif! They had placed these little red decorative sheets over the lamps. It was wonderful and so embarrassing. My wife still laughs about it today."

Keith and Margaret graduated from the university together. Margaret had arrived earlier and pursued an accelerated program of study, earning her master's degree in Communication Science in her fourth year. Keith earned his Bachelor of Arts degree in Speech Communication and Theater Arts. He applied to several graduate degree programs in communication and was awarded a teaching assistantship at a state school in northern California. Happy to return to the West Coast, Keith settled into a routine of coursework and work as a teaching assistant in large undergraduate classes in public speaking and argumentation, while Margaret taught at a local community college. He thrived academically in his graduate studies, maintained a grade point average of 3.80, and earned a Master of Arts degree in Communication Studies. During this period, the newlyweds became the parents of a baby girl.

The Early Career Years

Following several unsuccessful attempts at acquiring an academic position in his field, Keith decided to pursue opportunities in sales. He accepted a position with an academic publishing company in Memphis, TN, and enjoyed selling textbooks to university professors. Margaret found part-time employment teaching at an International Baccalaureate high school. Keith said, "I liked the idea of the publishing job because I'd get to stay in higher education and get to talk with professors all day. That was fun, but it wasn't fun because my job was to sell textbooks." This was a difficult situation for the family, as Keith spent so much of his time traveling and was away from Margaret and his young daughter. He began working for a different publishing house. His assigned territory was not as geographically spread, and he was able to be home regularly; however, the work remained much the same. He reflected, "I felt like I talked to people all day and never talked to a soul. It was lonely work. I'd arrive in a university town, and I never knew a soul." He arrived home from work one evening and announced to his wife, "I'm not happy. What do you think about me looking for a teaching position?"

Margaret agreed with the plan and supported him with the job search as he interviewed with three universities. His son was born a week before a scheduled interview. The proud grandparents had come to visit, so Keith's father accompanied him on the 9-hour trip through the Appalachian Mountains to the university for Keith's interview. He described his initial reaction to the community: "As we pulled into town, it was like entering an oasis from the rural, backwoods Neverland. It was beautiful and reminded me of northern California." He felt positive about the position and was impressed with the faculty. He later learned that he was the unanimous choice of the search committee because "the rhetoric people could talk to me because that was my training, and we had these business-oriented people who liked me because of my experience in sales and thought I would bring my real-world experiences into the classroom." Keith had planned ahead—he brought Margaret's résumé with him to the interview and inquired about part-time work for her. "Her teaching evaluations were out of this world, and her letters of recommendation were superb. So we were able to negotiate a dual-hire."

Keith was enjoying his third year at the university at the time I interviewed him. Margaret had moved from part-time employment to full-time and served as codirector of the debate program. With two young children, their schedules were packed. Both had a heavy load of teaching undergraduate classes they enjoyed. Margaret had initiated a series of monthly "Socrates Cafés," discussion groups open to the entire student body. Keith commented, "We think that college campuses should be environments where students can discuss big questions about life." He pointed out that the cafés had been an effective way to recruit students for classes and the debate team. Keith was responsible for the debate team, arranging for travels to multiple tournaments and managing the logistics. The team typically traveled five weekends each semester. They were pleased that the debate team had grown in numbers and were excited about hosting an upcoming national debate tournament on campus. They also hoped to eventually build a graduate degree program. In addition to their university work, they were both active in local and state politics and volunteered time in advocacy work for environmental and social justice issues. Keith recognized that he and Margaret were in a good place in their lives.

As we concluded our weeklong conversation, I asked him to share what he believed would be important lessons to pass on to my readers:

> I would hope that young men [who] weren't born in privilege and have a tough life recognize that my experiences are mine and their experiences are theirs. There may be similarities and differences, but nevertheless, there will be difficult situations to face in life. I hope that these young people recognize that their difficult experiences will never go away but to know that they don't destroy you, they should make you better, make you stronger. . . . I would also hope that teachers who read [this] book get the message that they make the difference. I wouldn't be here today if it were not for Mr. Warner, Mr. Eastman, Dr. Dow, Mr. Beale, and Dan Truman. I wouldn't be who I am. If there are young men out there who identify with my story, they can know that, no matter how dark and depressed they might feel, . . . there is light at the end of the tunnel. They have to understand that you get one shot at life. It's an interesting game, and it's what you make it.

Epilogue

Keith and Margaret enjoyed developing the debate program at the university for 4 years and moved on to direct debate programs at two additional universities for 3 years. Keith was recruited back to the publishing industry and is currently a regional sales manager for a large academic publishing house on the West Coast.

CHAPTER 3

DANTE

My work with Dante Medina began with an unsettling e-mail message. I communicated with all of the participants in my research through e-mail to schedule interviews. Early on in my conversation with Dante, I received the following message:

> Thank you for your message, Tom. I'll be at home this weekend, and you can reach me on my mobile. Suggesting a good time to reach me is somewhat of a difficult task because my feeling of wellness comes and goes, as last Friday I had bilateral anterior craniotomies to correct massive subdural hemorrhaging over my cerebral cortex, and I am recovering slowly at home. The onset of my symptoms was rapid, and the etiology of the bleeding is unknown. I will be convalescing for the next few weeks, but I believe I will still be able to participate in interviews. I look forward to your call.

I immediately contacted a close friend who was an experienced nurse. I needed her expertise to help me better understand Dante's situation. She quickly responded with, "The young man you are communicating with is lucky to be alive! I'm surprised he has been released from the hospital." She continued, "It's hard to say how long he'll need to recover. I'm guessing it will depend on whether or not the bleeding caused any brain damage."

In my response to Dante, I highlighted that I was praying for him and his recovery. I explained that his health came before anything else, and I did not want to conduct interviews while he was recuperating from his surgery. I promised to check in with him regularly, and we would arrange a time to meet when he was feeling stronger. A month later, in his correspondence with me, he shared the following:

> Thank you for your kind words. I appreciate your concern. I strive to not let anything get me down and see adversity and crisis as powerful agents charged with the energy to effect positive change. It is my good fortune to have that outlook on life. There is a Sanskrit phrase "Om Namah Shivaya," which loosely translates to "I embrace change" or "I bow before transformation." It is fitting for me and my current circumstances. I do look forward to meeting you soon.

Reading that message, I knew that Dante was a remarkable individual and wondered how he had acquired such internal strength. Weeks later he communicated with me to let me know that his recovery had been "surprisingly fast." He explained that he was still recuperating at home and going about his day "with little incidence, save for a lower energy level and occasional pressure on my forehead." He was happy to report that he had been cleared by his doctors to return to work at the beginning of the month and would be available for interviews. We agreed to meet that month, and I assured him that I would take into account his level of stamina in conducting the interviews. I moved forward with airline and hotel reservations.

At the time of the study, Dante was living in a large metropolitan city in the Midwest. When he provided me with the name of his neighborhood, I went online and researched the area of the city. I learned that it was the heart of the LGBTQ community. My flight travels were smooth and uneventful, and a cab took me to my hotel.

The hotel was several city blocks from Dante's neighborhood. Knowing that I would be meeting Dante the next day, I explored the area to get myself situated. After getting settled into my room, I went in search of a good restaurant for dinner and discovered a great Italian place. That evening as I walked the city streets, I noticed rainbow flags hanging in many storefronts. Dante had suggested that we meet at "the center" and provided me the address. He described himself and indicated that he'd be wearing a large hat and bright orange sneakers. I learned that "the center" was the LGBTQ community center. When I arrived in the lobby, I spotted him—Dante was 6 feet tall and thin. The large hat he was wearing covered heavy bandages from his recent surgery. He greeted me with a warm smile and a hug. We had agreed to conduct the interviews in a conference room at the center, but he explained that all of the rooms had been reserved by other groups. He suggested we conduct the interviews at his apartment. He assured me that he was comfortable with that arrangement, and it would actually be easier for him. I agreed to his plan. We walked several blocks to his home and enjoyed casual conversation about my travels to the city, the great cuisine I had enjoyed the night before, and the energetic quality of life in his neighborhood.

When we got settled in his apartment, Dante was gracious and made certain that I had a comfortable place on the living room sofa to conduct the interviews. After he served us hot tea, he situated himself in a large upholstered chair, wrapped himself in his favorite afghan, grabbed his mug, and prepared to share his life story with me.

Learning About Dante's Latest Challenges

We began by discussing his current situation. Several weeks before his surgery, he had interviewed for a position as the director of an Alzheimer's unit in a long-term care facility. He received a phone call from the administrator of the facility while he was in the hospital's intensive care unit. He was offered the position and was assured that they would hold onto the position until he was ready to return to work. When released from the hospital, he contacted the administrator and accepted the position. He had a letter from his neurosurgeon stating that he was okay to return to work with the restriction that he work no more than 8 hours per day. He was delighted that the facility's administrators had been impressed with him and insisted on holding onto the position for him.

He explained that he had just completed his third day of orientation and described his new job. He indicated that his work would include being responsible for the safety and well-being of 60 residents in various stages of dementia. He would oversee 30 nursing, housekeeping, and dietary staff and would be responsible for addressing the concerns of resident family members. He would also serve as the liaison between the physicians and the nursing staff and serve on all committees associated with the facility. He was excited about the position because his schedule involved no evening shifts, the salary was substantial, the facility was a pleasant environment, and he had done this type of work in the past. He explained his rationale for accepting the job:

> With my current health situation, for the first time in my life, I have had to step back and reprioritize. My life has always been about an upward trajectory—taking on more challenges and doing more, making more money, developing more skills, and taking on more responsibilities. Knowing that my total recovery is going to take several more months, I decided on this position. Even though it sounds like a stressful job, I can actually do this in my sleep.

Dante discussed how he saw similarities between his earlier work with children with developmental disabilities and his current dementia patients. "The approaches you take to communicate with them and problem solve are very similar." He assured me that he found great joy in this work:

> The most enjoyable aspect of the job are my patients, my residents. I find joy in a number of ways. The daily interactions with them, whether it's someone who is high-functioning and learning that they were once an accomplished pianist and being able to share that moment, or a lower functioning resident who hasn't spoken in years who says a word to me. That's kind of a breathtaking experience. I also find joy in the problem solving. Coming up with solutions to problems that concern family members. Nobody wants to put their loved ones in a nursing home, and there is often so much family dissatisfaction. To be able to problem solve and have a family member be reassured because I am there is so rewarding.

Dante divulged his long-range plan. He acknowledged that his new position would enable him to prepare for a professional move to the West Coast. He had long dreamed of living in San Francisco, and he explained:

> When I first come out to myself, I was 14. I knew I was gay when I was in second grade, but when I was finally okay with it and said out loud to myself, "I'm gay," I started really planning my life. I watched the miniseries called *Tales of the City* regularly, and I loved the idea of San Francisco. When I visited the city earlier this year, I got there and had the feeling that this was home. I loved the hills, the attitude of the residents. The weather was amazing. I love spring, and San Francisco has an eternal spring.

He had been planning this move for several years, but realized he needed to meet four criteria he established for himself before making the transition. He wanted to have earned his nursing license by endorsement with a year of experience, to have a nursing position lined up, a housing situation determined, and a substantial amount of money saved for the transition. He saw his current situation as temporary and looked forward to the future.

I asked Dante to share his recent experience with surgery. He described how he had a slight headache for several days. He assumed that it was simply stress-related, but one morning he woke up with the "worst headache of my life." When he discovered he also had high fever, he debated whether or not to go the emergency room. With his nursing background knowledge, he was attempting to figure out whether or not he was battling viral meningitis. When he was not successful in bringing his fever down, he arranged to have a taxi take him to a local hospital. By midnight, the emergency room staff administered a CT scan, and the doctor explained, "looking at the CT scan, we think you have blood on your brain, but we need to consult with a neurosurgeon; it may just be bacteria." Dante explained, "I immediately went into ICU and was hooked up to every kind of monitor and had all kinds of IVs started." The following morning the doctor explained that Dante had a subdural hemorrhage, and his only option for treatment was to have a craniotomy and have the blood drained from his brain. He provided the doctor his power of attorney documents and a list of phone numbers of people to contact. He explained:

> I spoke to him early in the morning, and he said, "I'll be back around 4:30 this afternoon, and you can give me your decision then." So I had to spend that day deciding whether or not I was going to live or die because it all goes back to quality of life.

As a nurse, Dante's knowledge of the medical field enabled him to understand the severity of his situation. He pointed out that of people who have subdural hemorrhages, 25% die within 3 hours of the craniotomy, 25% die within 2 days, and only 20% go on to live their normal functioning lives. He knew he had to make a decision quickly and was grateful for the doctor's reassurance when he said, "You don't have any neurological involvement right now. You're walking, you're talking, all your sensory and motor nerves are intact." When the doctor returned, Dante had made his decision:

> I called Elizabeth, my foster mother, and we had a long conversation. She said, "Dante, logically, you only have one option, you have to go through the surgery." I made the decision, they quickly wheeled me into surgery, and I woke up recovering from anesthesia in my room in ICU. . . . I was immediately hooked up to a patient-controlled anesthesia. Basically, it's a machine with buttons that I pushed whenever I felt pain and it had timers on it. I could push the button every 15 minutes and it would deliver 1.5 mg of morphine. There was no lockout. A lockout is a setting where they could limit the amount of morphine I could receive in a 4-hour period. That tells you just how much pain I was in.

Dante reflected on the many competent and kind nurses who were with him in ICU. His worst memory was the daily CT scan, having to transfer onto the machine as he was attached to monitors and the excruciating pain he felt when dealing with a bump in the hospital elevator. He laughed as he described the mullet haircut he received before the surgery and how he repaired it when he arrived home. He explained that the medical staff released him after one week. The surgeon pointed out that he would never experience another roller coaster ride. When he told the surgeon that he enjoyed inline skating, the doctor responded, "Wear a helmet!"

He talked about the many people who came to see him and was touched by the fact that they simply sat by his bed spending nighttime hours watching him sleep. From that experience, he learned who his real friends were. He pointed out that he celebrated his 31st birthday in ICU. He knew that he was young to have suffered a subdural hemorrhage, for they are more common in the elderly. He smiled as he said, "My friends have said it's because I have an old soul." He understood that he would need a long time to process the entire experience and said, "This experience is life-altering. It taught me that I'm extremely resilient." He posted his progress on his Facebook page to let friends know that he was returning to work, and many responded with astonishment as to how fast he was recovering. He pointed out that the spring weather made a difference for him: "Everything outside is starting to grow and blossom and heal itself. I'm going through the same process." He grinned as he reported to me that he had recently treated himself to an expensive birthday gift of new inline skates, and he was looking forward to the feeling of "exhilaration" he experienced when skating.

Dante's Early Childhood and Elementary School Years

Dante's earliest memory of his childhood was his mother's funeral when he was 4 years old. "The only thing that I remember for sure about my mother was seeing her casket and the priest sprinkling water on it. I was so young, and I didn't understand what was going on." He explained that he and his siblings were living in a border town in Texas with their mother at the time of her death. She was struck by an automobile as she was crossing the street and died instantly. She was 33 and was estranged from her husband, a gentleman from Mexico. Together they had five children. Dante pointed out that he had a copy of the marriage certificate; however, there had been questions regarding the validity of the document. He learned later that his father had entered the United States illegally and questioned whether or not his parents had been legally married. Following the funeral, Dante's aunt took Dante and his siblings into her custody. He explained the reason for this decision:

> Everybody asks, "Why didn't your father take care of you guys?" The reason my aunt came and took us was because during my grandfather's funeral, my biological mother and aunt had a conversation. They were best sisters; they had a very good relationship. My mother asked that my aunt take care of us children should anything ever happen to her. And so, on that promise, my aunt had custody of us. Texas Social Services had

no problem with it because my father was an illegal alien. They did not want us to go to Mexico. Apparently, it was a very easy process for her to simply take us. My Aunt Donna was 28 at that time, and she was living in a trailer, and she had her daughter. She was working as a forklift operator at that time. The trailer was small, and she really didn't have enough room for five more children, so my two older brothers went to live with [our] Uncle Gus. My uncle lived in another community about a 5-mile drive from the trailer park, so we were close enough to visit with each other frequently.

Aunt Donna had difficult decisions to make. Living with her daughter, Cindy, in a trailer was crowded, and she was now responsible for five additional children. Dante assumed that she chose to have his oldest teenage sister, Maria, live with her in order to help her with the younger children. His two older brothers, Paul and Sebastian, went to live with Uncle Gus because they could help him with his business. Dante's youngest sister, Magdalena, a child with developmental disabilities, also remained with Aunt Donna. Aunt Donna was involved in a relationship with a gentleman named Butch, an electrician she had met in her factory work, and together they found a house to rent for the larger blended family.

Dante's aunt eventually brought the children from the border town in Texas to a small lakeside community in a Northwestern state with a much less diverse population. His earliest memory of his transition was that of his first-grade teacher, who noticed that he was having difficulty in class and referred him to an audiologist. He was diagnosed as having a hearing impairment and received his first hearing aids, which he described as "these large over-the-ear type of things." He remembered the teacher introducing him to the class as an orphan who had been adopted. He described how the teacher read a picture book about an orphan and later another book about a young girl with a hearing aid. He said, "I think she was trying to make me feel comfortable, and she was also trying to make the other children understand. After all, I was the only child in class who was not White, and I arrived speaking some Spanish at that time."

Dante's vivid memories of second grade were mixed. He entered an art contest, and his poster was selected as the best of the entire school. He said, "I was legendary in the school for my art." He also remembered being bored in math and being reprimanded for working ahead in the math workbook. Although his computations were all correct, he was given a failing grade for not having followed instruction and felt humiliated. His situation improved in third grade when he encountered Mrs. Callahan:

> Third grade was when the magic started to happen. My teacher Mrs. Callahan was my favorite. She had a piano in the classroom, and every day we would sing the Pledge of Allegiance. She recognized my artistic talent. She saw that I was special in many areas. I just loved her. I was selected as Student of the Month, and at the end of the year, the class got to vote on Student of the Year. It was down to three students, and surprisingly, I was one of the candidates. I remember waiting outside the classroom while the rest of the class voted on who was going to be the star of the year, and then I won— Student of the Year!

Dante was rather astonished that he had been selected, because he felt he was always viewed as an outcast. He explained that he had a tightly selected group of female friends, and he dreaded any school activities that were organized by gender. He described his peer group situation and the verbal bullying he experienced:

> The popular kids definitely shunned me. The boys all shunned me, but at that time, I was a high achiever, I was on the school's safety patrol, I won the science fair, I always won the art competition, so everybody knew that I was really good at art. The same students who would call me "girl" on the playground would ask me to draw for them in classroom projects. I was verbally bullied and the verbiage, the language, evolved as we grew older. In the early years, it was "girl" or "sissy," and then I started hearing "faggot" in fifth or sixth grade, and it got even uglier . . . "homo," "queer."

Dante described the challenges with his peer group and also highlighted several of the most positive experiences he encountered. The science fair in third grade was a significant event, which Dante described as "really cool."

55

> I essentially discovered the scientific method.... I had observed mold and mildew, so my experiment was to determine under which conditions do mold and mildew grow fast.
>
> I had bread in jars. One was in the kitchen right on the windowsill, one was in a dark closet, and then one was someplace else. Then I had socks in plastic bags. I had the socks under the same conditions. I wrote about the mold and mildew, and I drew pictures of what they looked like on a microscopic level and I charted the progress every week. I kept notes of the progress of my experiment; I drew pictures of where the mold was and how much mold was there. I kept a journal of "I think this is happening because...." At the end, I presented my final results.

He pointed out that other students arrived with sophisticated looking presentations on display boards that looked to be the work of helpful parents. He had not prepared a display board, and when he inquired, he was told the judges were about to begin their review of the projects, so he decided to enter his work without a presentation board. He smiled as he reported, "I was awarded the grand prize for the entire school. I beat all fourth graders, third graders, and second graders. It was true science, and it was obvious that I didn't receive help from parents. I had the trophy."

He reflected on his last day of third grade when the classroom teacher's aide presented him with an impressive binder of drawing paper. He said, "It was the really expensive stuff, and it had special erasers and charcoal, and some colored pencils." He described how she quietly took him aside: "She told me that I had a God-given gift." She asked Dante not to tell the other children about this special gift. He kept their secret and spent the entire summer enjoying his art. Dante's creativity was recognized in other areas. He participated in annual inventing competitions in his school. In fifth grade, he entered three inventions in the Invention Convention:

> One was a device that would make the antennas on the top of houses look less gangly and more like a box. The second invention was a device that you wear around your waist to prevent getting wrinkles in your pants. I called it the "Waist Saver." And the other invention was a popcorn holder for the

movie theater with an insulated place where you could put your cola.

Dante won the district grand prize for the popcorn holder. He received a $25 savings bond from a community bank and was featured in the local newspaper. He also won the school district's public speaking competition for his original speech on racism and went on to second place in the regional contest. During this period, his talents in music were also discovered. He auditioned to sing in the school's Christmas pageant and was selected as a soloist. Because of his hearing impairment, he did not necessarily hear or understand the lyrics of a song; however, his teacher discovered he had a fine singing voice, a falsetto. He said, "I'd listen to [the] melody and harmony more than the words of the song." He also discovered a passion for classical music:

> My dream of becoming a classical musician began in fifth grade. I remember cleaning the bathtub, and I had my headphones on, and I changed the radio station and I came upon NPR, and they were featuring a Mozart concerto. I was just so impressed with it that I started to listen to classical music on a regular basis. I loved it because there were no words I had to struggle with.

His Aunt Donna had purchased a set of encyclopedias for the family, and he read them daily. It was there that he discovered photographs of various musical instruments. "I saw the picture of the bassoon and thought it was the most exotic instrument. It looked beautiful, and then when I heard the sound of it, it definitely confirmed for me that I wanted to play a bassoon."

The Middle School Years

Dante maintained that no one should ever have to experience the middle school years. By seventh grade he experienced serious peer aggression. He pointed out that there were several negative factors that made him stand out. He had a hearing impairment and wore hearing aids. As the tallest in his class, he physically stood out. He looked different from other students because of his Hispanic heritage, and his mannerisms were viewed as feminine. He experienced verbal bashing daily in the hallways and on the bus, and was humiliated when "the coolest boy in school" approached him at his locker and simulated anal sex with him while other students watched and laughed. Teachers remained oblivious.

Fortunately, with the transition to seventh grade, Dante began to excel musically. Mr. Kendall, the band director, nurtured his interest in playing a number of musical instruments and began Dante's training on the bassoon. Dante enjoyed a daily music class and was placing as first chair clarinet, first chair bass clarinet, and later bassoon and oboe.

Dante became involved in a stock market game competition facilitated by Mrs. Branford, the middle school's enrichment specialist. Following the team's successful performance at the regional level, the teacher approached him with an invitation to enter the gifted education program. Dante assumed that he had not been identified as gifted earlier because his standardized scores may have been borderline. Mrs. Branford encouraged him to join the class, and although his arrival in the program caused quite a stir amongst other students in the program, his creative talents were eventually appreciated. He said, "I'm an outcast in this school, and suddenly I joined their clubhouse." He began working on the program's Odyssey of the Mind competition and gained social capital amongst the students with his creative abilities. He said, "I put a lot of work into OM, made a huge contribution with my ability to build things and my artistic talent when it came time to draw murals." He continued, "so that helped to cool things off between me and the other students. I eventually became part of the team."

The creative outlets in Dante's life were therapeutic at this time because his situation at home was challenging. He explained that Donna's partner Butch was extremely racist and tossed racial slurs in his direction daily, referring to him as a "lazy Mexican." He said, "I did not have a good relationship with him. I was feminine, and we didn't have that toss-the-football-together relationship." Tensions in the home grew as Aunt Donna would discipline the children using extreme measures. "My aunt would grab my head and bang it against the tub. I remember her daughter Cindy describing how she would get so enraged with her that she would attempt to strangle her." Butch was also involved in the discipline. Dante described one incident when his aunt had insisted that her daughter not have a particular male friend in the home while she and Butch went out for dinner and a movie. She made the other children vow to not allow the young man in. When Cindy snuck her boyfriend in for a visit that evening, young Magdalena reported this. All of the children but Magdalena suffered consequences. Dante described:

> They actually used this big stick. It was approximately three and half feet long, about a quarter inch thick and they used it on us. The beating went on for so long. I remember her hollering, "You dare to defy me!" There were these bar stools that we were leaning over, and it got to the point that they were beating us so badly that we were hiding underneath the bar stools. That time we really had marks, and she kept us both home from school the next day. Cindy was so physically harmed that she had some mobility issues. I had a large handprint on my face, and my aunt told me to tell the teacher that I had fallen.

When this abuse took place, Dante went to a teacher whom he described as "an approachable person" and reported how he and his younger sisters were being emotionally and physically abused at home by his aunt and her partner. The school guidance department brought in Child and Family Protective Services, and the children were placed in separate foster homes. Eventually the family underwent a counseling program for several months, and slowly Dante and his siblings were returned to the home. After being removed from Aunt Donna and Butch for close to a year, Dante was hopeful that their situation would improve. "Initially I felt kind of reassured that because I had opened my aunt's eyes to what she was doing and was reassured that she wasn't going to verbally and physically abuse us anymore. The emotional abuse continued. I felt like a prisoner, but I channeled my energies academically. School was my only outlet." Dante also described how running had become another coping mechanism. As a 10-year-old he had joined his aunt in her marathon running practice and discovered that he was faster than she was. She provided him with a runner's log and he maintained a year-round running program. He described running as "one thing that saved me." He elaborated:

> It became a coping mechanism when the abuse got bad. From the endorphin perspective, the feeling good, the reward, and

the opportunity to think and reflect. Usually by the time I was done running, I had either solved a problem I was having at school or a paper I had to write. Or I would have pushed away the memory of another incident of physical abuse.

In seventh grade, he joined the track and field team at school and consistently won first place in the mile run. He enjoyed a supportive relationship with his track coach, and by eighth grade, his running skills were so advanced that he was allowed to join the high school team in their practices. He described the response of the high school students: "They were not supposed to like me because I have all these strikes against me. I don't look like them. I don't act like them. I'm smarter than them, and I'm not cool, yet I am cool because I'm their star athlete. It just added to the ambiguity."

During Dante's eighth-grade year, Aunt Donna and Butch decided to build a new house. While the house was being built, the family lived in two separate travel trailers. Winter was approaching, and the adults were stressed out over the construction. Aunt Donna was working a lot of overtime hours at a factory. Determined to have the sheetrock completed, the electrical wiring done and the carpeting installed, his aunt borrowed a huge sum of money to speed up the process. The children were put to work in assisting with the construction, and tensions in the family were high. Incidents of physical abuse increased. Dante commented:

> She was making about $30,000 a year, and Butch was an electrician so he made more significant money. I would say they were making $70,000 a year. So we had a swimming pool, an outdoor hot tub, and a 5,000-square-foot house. We had four vehicles and a Caterpillar tractor, but they didn't invest money in us. She would scream about having to pay for my clarinet lessons, and by middle school, I was expected to buy my own clothing.

The High School Years

The increasing tensions at home reached a peak when Dante's aunt discovered that he had been going online to visit a group for gay teenagers. Dante had posted his thoughts concerning whether or not he would ever be able to come out to his family. A member of the online community outed him to his household. Dante described his aunt's response:

> She was livid. There was some physical abuse, but it was mostly a lot of psychological and emotional abuse. I can't even begin to tell you the derogatory words she used to describe me. She would call me a child molester. . . . I was essentially grounded for life. I was not allowed to go out. I could only do extracurricular activities and come straight home. I could not receive any phone calls. I became a prisoner.

Dante did receive emotional support from Cindy during this difficult period. She introduced him to Scott, another gay teenager, who worked in a local convenience store. Eventually Dante would arrange to skip classes at the high school and meet up with Scott for lunch at fast food restaurants. Scott introduced Dante to the gay teenage community in a neighboring town, and shortly after, Dante had his first romantic relationship with Timothy. During this period, Dante had made a connection with another high school student while walking home from school. This young man was brilliant but very disenchanted with school and claimed he wanted to run away from home. As they walked home together, they traveled alongside the train tracks. This inspired Dante, and he spent 6 months studying the schedule of freight trains that traveled through his town. One evening Dante was watching a *Saturday Night Live* sketch with Adam Sandler that was poking fun at the Boy Scouts and their controversial stance on homosexuality. Dante explained that when Butch found him watching the show he went "ballistic" and "basically beat the crap out of me just because I was watching this TV show." That was the catalyst that triggered Dante into action. He knew that Donna and Butch would both be working the next day, and he had a plan:

> As soon as their vehicle drove out of the driveway, I was in high gear. I knew I had a small window of opportunity. I had already packed my gear. I found a hunting backpack in the storage shed, and I packed the essentials I would need. I was smart. A couple weeks earlier I noticed that the filing cabinet was unlocked, so I took my social security card and my birth

certificate. I knew I would need this stuff. There was no way I could run away without it. . . . By this time, Cindy had moved out of the house and was living on her own. Magdalena was alone watching TV downstairs and was oblivious to what I was doing. . . . My adrenaline was pumping, and I can remember a light dusting of snow. I remember walking down the driveway and noticing the smell of the snow. To this day, I can still hear the sound of the snow crunching under my boots. This is implanted in my brain. Our driveway was really long, but my magnetic pull was so strong. Once I hit the gate to Hunting Lodge Road, I had my freedom, and my life changed forever. It was so surreal. I walked 3 miles and managed to make it to the highway. I found a pay phone and called Cindy. She freaked out when she heard that I had escaped and came and picked me up in her boyfriend's Volkswagen Beetle, and she drove me to Timothy's home [in a neighboring community].

Dante's escape took place on Valentine's Day. He was 15. He referred to this event as his "Emancipation Day." He said, "This was the beginning of my life. I became confident. I freed myself. I earned my self-esteem." During this escape from home, he communicated only with Cindy and his high school guidance counselor to assure them that he was safe. His Aunt Donna reported him to the police as a runaway. Initially, Timothy introduced him to the gay subculture in a neighboring community, where he met many gay teenagers and eventually moved in with an adult couple, who provided shelter for him in their home for 3 months. With the legal documents he had packed, Dante was able to find employment as a dishwasher. When the couple made plans to move to another state, he moved into Timothy's garage. He communicated with his high school counselor, who explained that he had to be placed in the system with Child and Family Protective Services in order for anyone to be able to help him. He would have to return home. His high school guidance counselor arranged a meeting with his aunt and representatives of Child and Family Protective Services. Following the meeting, his aunt drove him to her daughter Cindy's apartment because she did not want him in her home any longer. He lived with Cindy for several months and then moved to a neighboring state to live with his older sister, Maria. During this time, he learned from his case manager at Child and Family Protective Services that he could receive a Social

Security income from his mother's survivor benefits and could cover his expenses with those funds. Missing his friends, he decided he needed to return home. With another phone call to his case manager, arrangements were made to return him to his community. Aunt Donna picked him up and took him back to the house where he spent the night. He had been gone for close to 6 months. He said, "The next morning my aunt threw my luggage out and said, 'Just go. I don't want you here. You're free to go.'" Again, he walked to Hunting Lodge Road, and a neighbor spotted him on the highway, picked him up, and drove him to the police station. The police communicated with his aunt, realized that she had abandoned Dante, and made arrangements for him to move into a children's shelter until a foster home situation could be determined. Dante was fortunate to be assigned two foster parents, Elizabeth and Jeff, who were both kind and supportive.

He moved in with his new foster parents and spent his summer enrolled in school to make up for lost coursework, having missed half of his sophomore year, and prepared for the upcoming court trial to have his aunt's guardianship terminated. She did not resist the termination of the guardianship, which enabled Dante to now become a ward of the state. He was relieved, as he realized that as long as his aunt was his guardian, he would still be under her control, and when it came time to leave for college, he knew that she was not going to provide for his education. He said, "I was already looking at colleges and reading college guides. I realized that applying for financial aid involves your guardian's tax information, and I knew she would resist."

He described living with Elizabeth and Jeff as "an incredible experience." They treated him like an adult from the first day, trusting him, providing him a flexible curfew, and remained concerned about his emotional well-being. He spent his entire junior year of high school with them. In July, they explained to him that they were moving to another state. They pointed out that he had three options: He could move to another foster home, move with them to their new community, or begin college early.

Dante believed that early entrance into college was the best plan. He easily passed the GED and began applying to colleges. He performed well on the ACT and was admitted to the state's flagship university. He was provided a full music scholarship, which paid for his tuition. He also was granted financial aid in Pell Grants and Stafford loans to cover the cost of his living expenses and room and board. With strong support from his case manager and strong letters of recommendation, Dante's early entrance into college from a foster home before the age of 18 was precedent-setting. His official move out of the foster care system took place on July 4—at this, he smiled and said, "Yes, the Fourth of July became my Independence Day. I have these two holidays that have special meaning, and I celebrate for myself. I don't really need fireworks nor do I care for the cliché of chocolate and roses on Valentine's Day, but I celebrate them."

The College Years and Graduate School

A friend of Dante's who owned a truck helped him move to the university for his freshman year. He arrived at his assigned dormitory ready to move in and was asked by the housing staff for his guardian's signature. He was only 17 years old and could not sign any legal documents. Fortunately, Dante had all of the court documents approving the plan for his early college entrance. When the housing staff reviewed the documentation from his case manager, they allowed him to move in. He smiled as he said, "So I signed on the dotted line, moved my belongings into the dorm, and started my new life."

Dante was grateful to his music teacher, Mr. Kendall, for having supported his plans for attending this university. Mr. Kendall was an alumnus of the university's music program and was delighted to send his star protégé to study with his mentor. Throughout high school, Mr. Kendall made sure that Dante was involved in regional music competitions, and Dante had the opportunity to meet and perform for Mr. Kendall's professional mentor, Dr. Agostini, an internationally acclaimed bassoonist. As a result, Dante was accepted into the music program with a significant scholarship package without having to audition. He thrived under Dr. Agostini and dedicated long hours of practice perfecting his bassoon performance.

He described his freshman year of college as "the most wonderful year" of his life. Dante finally found community. "I met so many people and created a great circle of friends that I still keep in touch with today." He described the university as the one liberal spot in the state with a vibrant gay community. He became involved in the LGBTQ community on campus and served as an officer in the group. He also became known across campus for his legendary performances in campus drag shows. Although he found his fellow music majors were more conservative, he enjoyed the camaraderie of the students and enjoyed his studies.

The summer following his freshman year, Dante remained in the university community and began a job working in a home for adults who are developmentally disabled. Having grown up with sister who is developmentally disabled, he had developed the skills needed for working in such a context. His title was "rehabilitation technician," and his responsibilities included a wide variety of tasks to keep the residents clean and safe. Dante continued this work part-time throughout his undergraduate years.

During his sophomore year, Dante decided he wanted to transfer to another school. He had applied to the state university at the time he and his case manager were having to negotiate a plan for early college entrance with the court system. He realized at that time that his precedent-setting case was a challenge and chose not to consider applying to out-of-state schools; however, Dante had long dreamed of studying music at a private liberal arts college outside of New York City. He applied and was invited to audition for admission. With support and a strong recommendation from Dr. Agostini, Dante flew New York and spent 2 days in meetings and an audition. When Dante met the bassoon professor, she asked, "Where are your parents?" Dante responded with "I don't have any parents." He said, "She seemed quite impressed by that, and then I played for her." After the 2-day experience on campus, he traveled to New York City and explored, went shopping, took in the Statue of Liberty, and decided that it was definitely the place where he wanted to be. "It was just as I had envisioned as an adolescent. The city was alive all day and night."

Shortly after his audition, he received notification that he had been accepted and would receive several scholarships that covered his full tuition. At the end of his sophomore year, he visited with Dr. Agostini, who gave him his blessing, and he said goodbye to many good friends who were happy for him but sad to see him leave. Dante looked forward to his new challenge. He had his personal belongings shipped and boarded a train to take him to New York. His new music school was larger, with more than 500 students and a higher caliber of talent. During his orientation week on campus, he made a decision to begin intense practice sessions on the bassoon. He described his early experience there:

> I decided that I would practice 5 hours a day. I practiced every single day during orientation week because I was preparing for ensemble assignments. There is orchestra, all of the bands, the wing ensemble, and the concert band. For bassoonists, the coveted position is principal bassoon of the orchestra. Keep in mind that I was considered a sophomore because of the way my transcripts had transferred. I had a sophomore standing, and I was competing with seniors and grad students. So I practiced and practiced. Dr. Agostini had trained me well, but I practiced to improve my tone and technique. I auditioned and received first chair, my first year there. I was awarded the principal bassoon seat. I was the star bassoonist, which changed the whole dynamic of my experience in music school. Suddenly other students wanted me to play in their chamber groups. I had graduate students approaching me and saying, "Dante, you have to play in my Woodwind quartet," or "I'm doing a recital, and I need a bassoon." So I was extremely busy playing for other students. I was bassoon boy. I was the star. Every year I auditioned for orchestral placement, I was awarded [the] principal seat.

Dante maintained that his program of study was rigorous, especially his music theory and music history courses. He enjoyed a variety of liberal arts classes and was positive about his experience, which earned him a bachelor's degree in music. He concluded his senior year with a visit to meet his father, who was living in a Midwestern state. Dante struggled to remember his father because Dante was so young when his father and mother were estranged. His aunt had taken custody of him and had "painted horror stories" about his father. He described his reunion:

> There were tears and more tears streaming down his face. He's very Mexican, so family is incredibly important to him. He kept saying, "My son, my son. I love my son!" He introduced me to all of his friends. I was surrounded by all of these Mexicans, and they were all speaking Spanish, and I didn't know a lick of Spanish. I felt out of place, but I was a celebrity. It was like a

homecoming. I understood that I had to accept him. I felt his love. I truly felt his love."

Several years later, his father passed away, and Dante remained grateful for the reunion and their time spent together.

During senior year, Dante decided to continue his studies in music and applied to several schools for a master's degree program. His preferred program was a prestigious school of music in New York City, and he dreamed of studying with Dr. Mancini, an internationally renowned bassoon artist and teacher. Dante had performed for him during a master class in his undergraduate program. Mancini had visited his school, and Dante had been selected to perform and be critiqued in front of a student audience. That experience had motivated him to apply to the Manhattan school to pursue his studies under the tutelage of this impressive musician. Following an intense audition, he received notification that he had been admitted with a merit scholarship. When fall arrived, he moved into the International House, a dormitory for graduate students from a variety of schools throughout Manhattan. His day-to-day experience was very intense academically; however, the emphasis of the program was on performance, which Dante claimed, "created an intense dynamic as far as how students interacted with each other and the faculty." He described the school's culture:

> Students who were identified as the most proficient musicians were highly praised by the entire school, and students [who] were lower on the ladder were either ignored, invisible, or shunned. I went from my undergraduate program where I was a star to now being the last chair. I was competing with people who had been playing bassoon since fifth grade, whose parents had paid for lessons since they were very young or had attended preparatory boarding schools in music. I had started playing in ninth grade. I was behind the game. That was a real shock and adjustment for me. I remember my first lesson with Dr. Mancini. I felt like an utter failure. I felt like he was probably thinking, "Why the hell did I accept this student?" But I came back for my next lesson, and he gave me high praises because it was apparent to him that I had spent a lot of time and work and contemplated all of his suggestions.

The music program involved real orchestra rehearsals in which the musicians would rehearse intensely for a week or two in order to produce regularly scheduled concerts. Students were required to audition each semester for their seat in the orchestra. Dante dedicated a minimum of 5 hours of practice each day and was delighted when he was moved to a much higher chair the second semester. He formed a support group of other students to deal with the intensity of the program and also developed a strong circle of gay friends to "hang out with" in Manhattan.

Under Dr. Mancini's expert guidance, Dante's skill and artistry on the bassoon opened opportunities to freelance with professionals in New York City. He networked with other musicians throughout the city and received invitations to play with a variety of groups. In addition to his freelance orchestral experiences, he participated in music outreach activities and was a frequent guest teaching artist at a music school for children on the Upper East Side.

His degree program also required a significant internship, and he interned for Chamber Music America's Bang on a Can, a premier New York performing ensemble for contemporary music.

He performed in nearly all of the major concert halls in New York, including Carnegie Hall and Lincoln Center. He also played with the Orchestra of the Bronx, and he was the principal bassoonist for the Conservatory of Music at Brooklyn College. He explained that all of these opportunities enabled him to network, build a resume, and gain valuable experience. He performed under the batons of many prestigious conductors. He shared his experience working with his idol:

> I played with Placido Domingo. He conducted a small ensemble from Argentina, and I was the bassoonist invited to play with them. He was naturally a pleasure to meet and work with, and we got to work very intimately because the group was very small, less than 15 musicians. He was very humble and very warm even though he was surrounded by all of these people who wanted to meet him. When I was talking with him, he truly devoted all of his attention and focus on me. It wasn't like he was just signing an autograph and moving on. He gave me a lot of compliments about my playing, my musicality, and my solos. That was most flattering.

After an intensive 2-year experience in Manhattan, Dante successfully completed his final graduate recital and earned his master of music degree with distinction. With his new partner, Robert, he moved to the Midwest and completed two semesters of coursework in music therapy. He was disenchanted with the program, and when a friend from his music program in Manhattan contacted him about an opportunity playing bassoon for an orchestra in Yucatán, Mexico, he decided to apply for the position. With application materials, a letter of recommendation from Dr. Mancini, and an audio recording of his performances, he was hired as the coprincipal bassoonist in the Yucatán Symphony Orchestra. He described his experience:

> I underwent culture shock. My inability to speak Spanish certainly limited my experience. Fortunately, there were several members of the orchestra who spoke English, and I had access to an English library. My typical routine was getting up before 8:00, rehearsing with the orchestra for 2 hours, having some espresso at a nearby Italian restaurant, and chatting with some of the orchestra members. I went home and slept in my hammock and had a siesta until 5:00, and then I'd have the whole evening to socialize with friends. I did study Spanish, and I picked up some Spanish just being immersed the culture, and of course, there was always time devoted to practicing. Overall, it was a mixed experience. The climate was incredibly oppressive. I was constantly soaked, and I had chronic gastrointestinal issues as I struggled to find food that I could eat.

His partner, Robert, was the manager of a luxury travel agency, and after 5 months in Yucatán, Robert arranged for a first-class airline ticket to return Dante home to the States. By this time, Robert had moved to a major metropolitan city in the Midwest. Dante was happy to join him, and he immediately began looking for work. He was hired as an activity director in a nursing home. Administrators were impressed with his music experience and promoted him to serve as director of the dementia unit. He enrolled in a community college and began taking courses in anatomy and physiology, as he had plans to apply to an innovative graduate nursing program at the local university.

Dante had become disenchanted with the professional orchestral world. "While I was playing with great orchestras and playing under the baton of great conductors, I had to spend long hours of practicing, and the work was not lucrative." He explained:

> I took several orchestral auditions where there were 10 bassoonists who were vying for this one position that only paid $30,000 a year for a subpar orchestra. There were older musicians in their mid-30s who trained at Juilliard [who] were auditioning. I thought that was sad, and I was very discouraged by this. I thought it was ironic that my liberal arts degrees would now actually confine me to where the jobs would be. I could end up stuck in Alabama or Tennessee or other very undesirable places, whereas in nursing, I could go anywhere in the world and be a nurse. The need for nurses is so high. If I wanted to move to England and be a nurse I could, or [I could] move to any city in the United States and work as a nurse.

Dante's decision to pursue a different profession did not occur overnight. Throughout his undergraduate years, he had worked in health care, and each position he took on involved serving individuals with developmental disabilities, work that he felt was very important. During his time in Manhattan, the events of September 11 occurred, and he spent many sleepless nights during that horrific period. He spent long hours online exploring nursing degree programs and contemplating his future.

Dante was admitted to a graduate nursing degree program at a major university and was stunned when he was awarded a merit scholarship from the Board of Trustees. "When that happened, I knew I was back on track." His nursing degree involved a 16-month accelerated program that was rigorous. The first half of the program was strictly nursing education, pharmacology, and physical assessment to prepare students for the National Council Licensure Exam, the nursing boards. He was one of four males in a cohort program he described as "a pressure cooker." With Robert's support, he studied furiously and excelled in his program. Upon completion of his master's degree in nursing, he began studying religiously for his national board exams and passed on his first attempt. He provided his rationale for becoming a nurse:

I have always advocated for the underdog, and that's why I'm a psychiatric nurse, because I am drawn to the weakest members of society, those who are most shunned. Within the nursing profession, the "cool nursing" may be the ER nursing, the kind of high-adrenaline work that's seen as glamorous on television. At the bottom of the profession is psychiatric nursing because so few want to work with all those crazy people. I have a great deal of empathy for them. My experiences with my younger sister, Magdalena, watching her struggle with growth and development and seeing the way people treated her has sensitized me to people with disabilities, be it physical, mental, or developmental. I also believe that my empathy comes from being a survivor of racism, being a survivor of gay bashing, being a survivor of adverse child abuse. My experiences have made me sensitive and enabled me to empathize for all of those populations.

Epilogue

Following the completion of his nursing degree, Dante worked on an interdisciplinary medical team that planned and implemented care for elderly adults with dementia in a specialized long-term care facility. He transitioned to several other institutions, working as a registered nurse. He reached his dream when he later moved to San Francisco to practice nursing. He is currently employed in a large metropolitan hospital in the Midwest. He is a registered psychiatric nurse providing treatment for patients with acute mental illnesses.

CHAPTER 4

SEBASTIAN

On a sunny day in April, I traveled through picturesque southern Appalachian mountains to a scenic university community to meet Sebastian Tucker. I arrived to discover a beautiful campus of 20,000 students. The university was home to many nationally ranked academic programs, including a highly respected academy for mathematics and science, which served as a residential high school for exceptional high school juniors and seniors. Sebastian, an academy alumnus, was the youngest participant in my research study, and he was in his second undergraduate year at the university, pursuing a double major in mathematics/secondary education and biology.

He and I had exchanged cell phone numbers in our earlier e-mail conversations. After extended "telephone tag," we succeeded in determining a time to meet at the university library for our first interview session. He arrived carrying notebooks and several thick textbooks from his afternoon classes. As we greeted each other, I was struck by his soft-spoken demeanor and warm smile. A tall, thin, young Black man dressed in an oversized sweatshirt and jeans, he was reserved and polite during our conversation. He led me to the front desk, where he chatted with the staff about the quiet conference room he had reserved for us. As I observed the interaction, I realized that Sebastian was well-acquainted with the library personnel. They knew this studious undergraduate student well from his daily visits for long hours of quiet study.

As we settled in, we chatted about the sunny weather, the beauty of the surrounding countryside, and the welcoming atmosphere of the campus. From our e-mail correspondence and cell phone conversations, I was aware that he juggled a busy schedule of classes and extracurricular activities, and I therefore appreciated his willingness to be involved in my study. I questioned him about his daily schedule, and he noted that his alarm clock rang at 5 a.m., so that he could have a one-hour workout in the university fitness center, followed by breakfast, before his morning classes began at 9 a.m. Classes and meetings filled up his day until late afternoon. Evenings involved long study hours that lasted into the early morning hours. With an 18-credit semester of courses that included a math course in differential equations, microbiology, computer science, an honors American government class, a course in African American studies, and a seminar class in secondary education, Sebastian explained that he needed the morning time at the gym for stress relief. He joked that he enjoyed an action-packed day and pointed out that since leaving home and having access to the fitness center, his morning workout had resulted in a weight loss of 50 pounds. He smiled as he noted this accomplishment, which had resulted in many positive comments from old high school friends. He seemed at ease during our casual chatting, and I was confident that my time with him would continue to be enjoyable.

Sebastian is an intelligent young man from an impoverished background who arrived at the university after many years of family turmoil. In his rural home community in south central Appalachia, population 4,200, approximately one-third of the population lived below the poverty line. As we met in the university's impressive library from day to day, I remarked to myself how far-removed Sebastian was from the difficult environment he had come from. Looking like a typical college student, his casual outward appearance camouflaged the struggles of his adolescence. I gradually understood why he seemed so content in the quaint and tidy university community.

Early Childhood and Elementary School Years

Sebastian's parents married in their mid-20s and had three children. He was the oldest. He was joined by Jocelyn, his younger sister by 2 years, and Natalie, 5 years younger. Both parents were high school graduates. His father had been employed in an automotive parts manufacturing plant, and his mother had been employed in nursing home care. Sebastian explained that the family lived in a small, rural brick home, and they enjoyed the bucolic environment. He reflected fondly on quiet summer days when he and his sisters played under the water sprinkler to stay cool.

However, some of his fondest early childhood memories were associated with his maternal grandmother, who lived nearby and dedicated much of her time to teaching her young grandson how to cook. He reported, "She loved to cook and we'd spend hours in the kitchen together. I was only 6 or 7, but she showed me how to do the basic things that I would need to know when I grew up." Sebastian grinned as he explained that he saw himself becoming a chef one day. This quality time in the kitchen with his grandmother continued. He smiled again when he said, "She continues teaching me to this day. When we go out there for gatherings, like Thanksgiving or family reunions, I'm there in the kitchen helping her with preparations. While everyone else is playing or socializing, I'm my grandmother's assistant in the kitchen." He also had a close relationship with his maternal grandfather when young. His grandfather coached baseball and involved Sebastian in a T-ball league, which he enjoyed throughout his elementary school years.

Sebastian had a loving relationship with his mother. Mrs. Tucker was born with cerebral palsy, and her life with a disability challenged her family in significant ways. He had great respect for her, evident when he described her situation:

> When she was a teenager, she underwent a major surgery. I don't know the logistics, but the surgeons went into her foot and her ankle and did some sort of meticulous manipulation to get her to where she could walk. She wore a brace for many years. She now walks with somewhat of a limp, but it's rather

> difficult to distinguish that she's disabled. What upsets me is when people know that she's disabled. I can see people talking to her like she's an idiot. At times, I'll get really furious, and even if it's a professional person, I have no problem interrupting the conversation saying, "She does understand you, and you are getting on my nerves." They think she doesn't know what she's talking about. I get so upset when they talk down to her.

Mrs. Tucker's disability occasionally impeded her employability, yet Sebastian emphasized that he respected her: "Even though she's disabled, she doesn't see the point of just sitting around when she's capable of working. She feels like she's not going to let this burden hold her down. That's why I really admire her." He learned how to deal with the community's view of her. When he saw that friends noticed his mother's disability, he was protective. He explained, "If they had something to say about it, I would handle them. She was my mom, and I was proud of her. They can think what they want to think, and I maintain that attitude even today."

The Tucker family's challenges evolved early in Sebastian's childhood and were driven by his father's alcoholism. Sebastian maintained that his father was absent for much of his childhood, and when he was around, his relationships with his wife and children were troubled. Sebastian described the drama revolving around his father's problem:

> My dad would get violent, and we'd have to go to my grandmother's house. We were always on the run. That part of my life was so dark, and I felt like I was at such a loss. I didn't want to be there. I didn't see the point of being alive. I just wanted to die. He'd get violent, and we'd have to leave the house quickly and run somewhere. I kept thinking, "Why do we have to live like this?" It just didn't make sense to me.

Sebastian explained that his father would often remark that because his wife had a disability, no other man would ever want her. Sebastian said, "He played with her mind. I think he argued that she would not be able to survive without him." Although he was able to reflect on early memories of his father reading him bedtime stories as a young child, Sebastian maintained that his father's problems with alcohol diminished many aspects of his childhood. He provided a description of a family shopping excursion:

> He would usually be drunk shortly after cashing his paycheck, so we took advantage of it. He'd say, "Get whatever you want!" So, hey, you tell a kid to get whatever they want . . . My sisters and I were putting all kinds of stuff in that shopping cart! Nonetheless, it was still embarrassing the way he conducted himself. We'd be shopping, and he would cuss out loud and he would degrade my mother. . . . He had a reputation in the county for the way he conducted himself—going downtown, acting like an idiot, and cussing.

With extreme difficulties at home, Sebastian chose to focus on doing well in school. His reflections on his elementary school years were positive. He described a number of encouraging teachers who responded to his conscientiousness. He shared how he grew to despise the Accelerated Readers program and how reading for points squelched his desire to read. He laughed as he gave examples of how he aggravated one teacher with his enormous, distinctive penmanship to the extent that the teacher complained about his using up the classroom supply of paper. The academic highlight of his early school years was mathematics, where he excelled. He described times when he and several others in his primary grade classes received enriched instruction in math.

Because Sebastian's family lived in an isolated area of the county, there were no neighborhood friendships. Friends at school became important. He described himself as initially shy, but when other children became acquainted with him, he was rather extroverted and occasionally enjoyed being the center of attention. He reflected on a personal characteristic that caused him trouble:

> I had this loud, hilarious laugh. My friends said it sounded like a horn going off. My friends found it hysterically funny, and that was something they liked about me. They would always try to get me laughing in class. My fourth-grade teacher sent me out to sit in the hallway a number of times for disrupting the class with my loud laugh.

Middle School

The middle school years academically were quite positive for Sebastian. However, he pointed out that his school experience during this period was influenced by the No Child Left Behind movement in public schools. He believed he was being held back and could have progressed with more acceleration. He explained that he did not enjoy collaborative projects because he preferred to work independently:

> I'm a perfectionist. I'm the type of person to say, "Give me what I need, and I'll just do it myself." I'm an independent person, because when my grade depends on the actions of somebody else and their responsibility, and they don't hold up their end, that affects me. Just let me do what I have to do.

Because his learning style was characterized by independence and personal effort, he believed that his sixth-grade math program was beneficial. He reflected on this with a laugh:

> We had this program called accelerated math whereby we worked at our own pace. It was computer-driven. You printed out material, and you got these worksheets. You'd scan your answer card, and you'd get your results. It was actually a pretty cool program, but it really killed a lot of trees.

Sebastian reflected on a number of teachers in middle school who recognized his abilities and strong motivation. He worked especially hard for teachers who were passionate about their subject area and took a personal interest in their students. He developed a personal strategy to build positive relationships with his teachers:

> I worked hard, and my teachers appreciated my character. I sat in the front row in pretty much every class so I made sure the teacher knew I was there. I made my presence known. . . . Naturally, I was often known as the teacher's pet, and I did suck up, but I also backed it up with hard work. I was a hard-working student, but I also enjoyed talking with my teachers and running errands for them.

Sebastian's social experience during the middle school years included some difficult challenges. He was one of five African American students among 190 students in his class. In this setting, he encountered what he described as "verbal abuse from redneck racist Southern White boys" in his community. He reflected on one particularly painful situation:

> I remember in my eighth-grade year being called the N-word in front of the entire eighth-grade math class. I was running an errand for my science teacher, and I went into this classroom, and one student called the word out loud. The teacher stopped the class, looked at him, and said, "Why did you say that?" She sent him to the principal's office, and he ended up getting suspended for the week. I thought he should have been suspended for the rest of the year.

Sebastian was forced to negotiate these difficulties at school, but he also had to deal with horrific challenges at home as the Tucker household became more and more problematic. He indicated that during this period his father's problem with alcohol intensified, and he became more abusive. Sebastian described painful scenarios:

> I remember trying to figure out if we were going to make it to the next day without him hurting one of us. I stayed locked up in my room and tried to avoid him, and there were times when I would just come in and crawl up in my bed and put my head under my pillow and try to fall asleep. He was just so unpredictable. I remember sitting in my room and hearing him blaring his music outside in his Explorer in the dark with the headlights on. My sisters and I were peeking out the window to see if he was coming in the house. We ran to our rooms and hid. . . . There was one time he cracked the window in his Explorer, and he tried to blame it on us. He didn't realize what he had done, and he was never remorseful. The next day he would just go on as though nothing had happened.

He and his siblings were forced to take a defensive approach:

> During my mid-teenage years, I started bonding more with my younger sisters. My dad would drink heavily and argue more with my mother. Occasionally he'd be violent and would strike

her. My sisters and I knew that we had to pull together and stay strong—to actually fight back with him. If he was getting ready to hit her, we'd take him down. My sisters would position themselves in front of my mom. My mother didn't want us to get involved, and we just couldn't get through to her that she needed to separate from him to have a more healthy environment for us.

As the oldest in the family, Sebastian pleaded with his mother to leave his father. He explained, "Disciplinary-wise, we took over. I felt awful about that, but then again what they were putting us through was completely uncalled for." He announced to his mother that he could not continue living like this and threatened to call the Department of Social Services to have him and his sisters removed from the home. She responded with tears and cries of "I don't want to lose you." Sebastian reflected on his siblings' different approach to the home situation:

I knew that I needed to get out of that environment. Even though I was doing good academically and trying to make something of myself, why were they not appreciating that enough to provide us a good environment to thrive in? My sisters and I responded so differently. We went on different paths. When my dad would beat my mother, they would go hang out with people who smoked pot, and I would stay there with my mom and help her get through it. They'd be running off. I still cannot understand how the three of us living there in the same environment responded so differently . . . my sisters wouldn't want to follow me, to make something of themselves, to get out of this situation, to get out of that community.

High School

Sebastian recognized his math talent in high school. He thrived in this subject area and soon developed quite a reputation in the math department. He earned a grade of 100 in Algebra I in ninth grade. At that time, he thought, "This math thing is really working out for me. I'm going to take more honors math courses." He moved on to Algebra II and had a final average of 97. He enjoyed precalculus and trigonometry with one of his favorite teachers, whom he described as "wild." He said, "She was a woman who said some of the most outrageous things during the first period of the day. Trig was my thing, I was ready to get going in her class, and I earned a 100 in that course."

Sebastian was involved in the Upward Bound program in his district, a federally funded program designed to provide fundamental support to high-potential students from underserved low-income backgrounds to prepare them for college entrance. His aunt had called his attention to the program and encouraged him to consider it. He applied, was interviewed, and gained admission. He benefitted from weekly meetings designed to provide students training in time management and study skills and to help them begin thinking about college. Upward Bound students also could participate in academic programs on Saturdays at the university. As a participant, he could also engage in a summer residential program on campus during his freshman and sophomore years. He was one of 17 students from surrounding county school districts who lived in a college residence hall and enjoyed cafeteria food, the camaraderie of other talented students, and the summer enrichment classes. He reflected on his response to the context: "Usually the guys were the type who didn't study. They liked to stay up late and not go to class, but that wasn't me. I was in bed by 10:30 p.m. and I did what I needed to do." He also pointed out that he benefitted from his relationship with the Upward Bound director, who later helped him with scholarship applications and negotiating federal financial aid paperwork. He explained, "Ms. Gaston was always checking up on me. I was one of her top students. Like a lot of my teachers, she knew how hard I worked, and she let me know how successful I was going to be in the future."

Because his father refused to transport his son to events at the high school, involvement in extracurricular activities was a challenge; however, Sebastian decided to audition for the color guard of his high school's marching band. He was one of two males in the color guard, and he acknowledged that the other young man was far more athletic than he was. He also indicated that being involved in this activity did not earn him any social capital. Other students questioned his sexual orientation, and he was regularly taunted with homophobic remarks; however, he explained his rationale for involvement: "I'm an intense person. I'm competitive, and I like the performance. I'm an open person, and I like to express myself. The color guard enabled me to do this in ways that were acceptable." Sebastian and I chatted about the high-energy movie *Drumline*, a film that depicts the fictional story of the North Carolina A&T State University Blue and Gold Marching Machine and its drumline. He commented, "That was a phenomenal movie. I was amazed at how intense the music was. It made me wish I had been involved in that. I'm an intense individual, so the more intense the better."

During Sebastian's junior year, his physics teacher, Ms. Bowden, approached him with a brochure about the newly established academy for mathematics and science at the university, which would be opening its doors to qualified high school students for the first time. Sebastian's life changed that day. He described his response to the brochure:

> I was amazed. I was absolutely astonished at how lucky I could be that my senior year fell right at that time. Had they opened one year later, I would have missed it. To this day, I just wonder who was watching over me, saying, "This is such a wonderful opportunity, just take it!"

With the support of Ms. Bowden, he was able to complete his application packet, which included letters of recommendation from math and science teachers, an English teacher who could speak to his writing abilities, and a fourth letter-writer he could select himself. Sebastian chose to have his counselor write on his behalf. He described her letter:

> Her letter centered on the fact that I'm just a loving person. I accept people. I'm fun to be around. She thought that I would thrive in that environment. She commented on how I excelled in my classes, and she thought the academy would be the perfect experience for me.

He chose not to discuss his application with his parents until the last minute. He explained, "I filled out the application, handed it to my mother and said, 'I need your signature,' and I was on my way." He provided his mother with a short description of the program, but he commented to me that she did not realize how significant it would be. He explained, "I didn't go into detail about my moving there for my senior year of high school. I didn't fully explain it to her until I received my letter about the interview with the admissions committee."

When Sebastian received word that he was scheduled for an on-campus admission interview, the Tucker family was without a vehicle. Ms. Gaston, his Upward Bound teacher, volunteered to drive him and his mother to the university. He described the interview:

> I was very nervous. The interview was with the director and another faculty member. They asked questions like, "What would you bring to the academy?" and "If you could design the academy, what three things would you be sure to include?" I remember I said "good food," and they laughed, and then it dawned on me that I'd made a foolish remark, but they agreed with me and laughed, so I just went with it. I talked about a comfortable living environment and an academically challenging program. As far as what I would bring to the school, I talked about my being motivated and fun to be around, because I think it's hard to find someone who's intellectually gifted and also has fun on the side. I explained that I was a mix of both.

Sebastian was concerned that he might not qualify. He had taken the ACT in his junior year, but was disappointed with the results. He believed that standardized test scores were not the best representation of his abilities and that his academic success was driven by his hard work and motivation. He was excelling in all of his math and science courses and hoped that the academy would recognize his strengths and consider his strong grade-point average and excellent letters of recommendation. Several weeks following the academy interview, he received an official letter of admission. He did not hesitate to sign his letter of commitment. He described the response of the faculty and his high school friends:

> When I received my acceptance letter to the academy, I took it to the office the next morning and showed my counselor, and she announced it to the whole school. After first period, Mrs. Smith, another math teacher I would have taken for AP Calculus as a senior, saw me walking down the hall and she called out, "Look here! Sebastian is going to the Academy, everybody!" It was awesome. I felt so prestigious.

He pointed out that several friends struggled with his decision to leave. He explained, "They carried on . . . 'Sebastian, we're going to miss you, you're always so excited. Who are we going to have to cheer us up next year?' and stuff like that. But they were happy for me." He decided he wanted to have social time with his teachers before he left school, and he therefore organized a luncheon. He explained, "I just asked them if they would want to get together for lunch. I wanted to say goodbye and thank them for everything they had done for me." He described the event:

> We actually held it at school, and everyone brought food. We went to my Spanish teacher's classroom while everybody else went to lunch. I invited my best friend, all of my math teachers, my Spanish teacher, my English 10 teacher, who actually brought along Mrs. Carter, who I was so looking forward to taking for my AP English my senior year. I also invited our principal, but he wasn't able to make it. We all had lunch and talked and just had a good old time. . . . Later I got each one of them a card, and I wrote a nice letter and gave it to them.

Late in the summer, the university offered a preview day for the families of the students accepted into the inaugural class of the academy. The construction of the academy dormitory was nearly complete. Sebastian described his reaction to seeing his new home, a state-of-the-art facility: "My mother and I came and saw it, and we were just . . . I don't even know how to explain it. It was like a castle! I had never lived in such good housing in my life."

However, although events in his academic life were positive, Sebastian's family life had become even more tumultuous. Mr. Tucker's employment at the automotive parts factory was terminated, his drinking increased, and tensions at home worsened. Sebastian pointed out that he and his sisters were directed by their grandmother not to escape to her house any longer. He explained, "I didn't blame her because my father would come out there and get her blood pressure up. Her doctor told her to stay away from what was going on with us. Otherwise, she was going to die."

When they were unable to pay the mortgage on their home, Mrs. Tucker and her three children moved into a federally subsidized housing community in the city. At this time, Sebastian's mother found the strength to separate from her husband. He moved to the Midwest. Mr. and Mrs. Tucker have been separated permanently since he left the state.

Life at the Academy

When Sebastian arrived at the academy, from a rural community where he had been one of five African American students in his entire high school, he discovered that he and an African American female were a "minority of two" in the new senior-year Academy cohort of 54 students. The third culturally diverse student was Asian. The demographics of the group did not trouble Sebastian. He reflected on the arrival of the inaugural class: "We came in, it was the first year ever, and we bonded. We knew we had to make it together, and we became a family." Many of the academy students remained at the university for their undergraduate years, and friendships continued. Sebastian admitted that initially he was somewhat intimidated by some of his academy peers. He described his initial impressions and how his view changed:

> I thought they all seemed so smart, and so many were coming from prestigious schools. I was here from a small county school. I was the only student from my county to even get accepted to this program, and I thought for sure they were going to rip me to shreds academically. They were so much more sophisticated, and they presented themselves well. Once I got to know them and live with them, I realized what you see is not always it. Living with them in the dorm I figured out they're not much different from me. I learned quickly that I was ripping them to shreds! So that shows how much hard work pays off. Many of them came here thinking, "Because I'm smart, I don't have to study." I came here thinking, "Okay. I'm given this opportunity. Let's see how much I can grab of it."

Friendships at the academy evolved naturally. Sebastian enjoyed his peers in the cohort: "The people I hung out with were as dedicated as me. They were all high-achieving, working towards the same goals." He pointed out that his friends often commented on how easygoing and happy he always was. He realized that leaving the conflict-ridden situation at home enabled him to be more relaxed; however, with his new friends he was honest about his home situation:

> When people asked, "Sebastian, how are you managing to do so well academically?" that would bring up my life story. I shared some details of my alcoholic father. I explained that after what I had gone through at home, I had to push myself to get out of that situation, so that's why I was working so hard. They then understood why I was so happy.

As an academy student, Sebastian benefitted from dual enrollment, whereby he earned college credit during his final year of high school while simultaneously completing required courses for a high school diploma. To determine his program of study, he was required to take an online math placement examination to establish whether he should be enrolled initially in college trigonometry or calculus. He was also required to complete three core science courses, and he chose to enroll in chemistry, physics, and two classes in biology. In addition to the math and science emphasis, he needed to fulfill the state's graduation requirements. Therefore, courses in English, art, and physical education were also part of his academic agenda. He met the academic standards of the academy and proudly reported that he graduated with a grade point average of 3.82. He had developed a friendly relationship with his resident counselor and enjoyed campus social events with undergraduates; however, the majority of his social activities centered around good times with his "academy family."

Academy students could return home for weekends, and many spent that time with their families. Sebastian often found himself practically alone in the dormitory on weekends, as he was content to be far removed from home. The situation with his sisters had become worse. They were both causing more problems for his mother. After the move to the housing complex in the city, they began associating with disreputable teenagers from the community, and Mrs. Tucker was distraught. When Sebastian attempted to intervene for his mother, they would scream, "You're not our dad. You can't tell us what to do!" Both sisters began skipping school. At one point, they disappeared for 3 days, and after frantic calls to the local police and a search of several counties, the authorities found them in a neighboring community. Eventually, after interventions by the Department of Social Services, the two girls were taken into state custody and placed in separate foster homes.

Although his family situation was difficult to negotiate during his year at the academy, Sebastian remained focused on his goals. His life at the academy became his salvation as he psychologically removed himself from the troubles at home. He knew that it was time to consider his postsecondary plans. He was fortunate to have the assistance of the academy's director. He described his college planning and application process:

> After all that time in my grandmother's kitchen, I had full intentions of attending the Culinary Institute of America in New York. I applied to the culinary arts management program to become a chef. I got accepted, but the tuition rate was $30,000 per year. Everybody was blown away that I'd been accepted, and when I received the acceptance letter I was thrilled, but then I had to start planning for financial aid. I received a substantial scholarship from the Culinary Institute, but it was not enough to cover the total expense. The academy director and I figured it all out. He really wanted me to go, but we figured I was going to have to take out quite a few loans. We discussed it often, and he said, "It's up to you. If you really want to pursue this and it's your passion, the debt won't seem as much of a burden, but it's all up to what you want." Essentially the thought of that amount of debt overwhelmed me. My parents had always been in debt, and I was determined to not be in that situation, so I decided to take the math route. I was successful in math, so I decided to apply to the mathematics program at the university. I decided on mathematics in secondary education with a minor in biology.

The academy's director helped Sebastian pursue financial aid to attend the university. With a combination of federal and state grants and a university scholarship through the minority teacher recruitment center, Sebastian would be able to attend college debt-free. He applied to the university and was admitted. He pointed out that he never regretted his decision:

> Since I've been at the academy, I have built so many relationships with professors and administrators. I even know the president and his wife. I will chat with them whenever I see them on campus. She's always excited to see me. She's thrilled that I'm here. She says she's ready to get me prepared for graduate school. . . . So many people were saying to me, "You have such good relationships built here, why would you want to leave?"

Sebastian also realized that if he pursued undergraduate studies at the university, as an Academy alumnus he would automatically be accepted into the Honors College, which would enable him to enroll in smaller classes known for rigor and dedicated student engagement. He also viewed this as an opportunity to immerse himself in his chosen disciplines, mathematics and biology. For his senior capstone thesis, he planned to strategically combine his personal passions and career goals in a research project he knew might influence future graduate study. The Honors College had great appeal. He believed the program would help to connect him to people similar in motivation, aspirations, and work ethic, who would also become important friends.

As his senior year at the academy was coming to an end, Sebastian returned home for his senior high school prom and graduation. He smiled and said, "I walked across the stage and received my diploma. I felt like quite the celebrity, and I sucked up all the glory. I felt I deserved it." He then went on to discuss the conclusion of his senior year. He described his second commencement day—the academy graduation:

> That was the epitome of my entire senior year. That was the best graduation ceremony I ever attended in my life. We were all in our academic robes and we were all lining up and I was about to cry. It was outside in the amphitheater, and it was so beautiful that day. We were all lining up, and I said, "This is it. We're all leaving!" And I walked across the stage to get my diploma, and I don't know, I just can't explain it. It was just this ecstatic feeling that overtook me. Everybody was so proud of me. My year at the academy flew by, because I arrived in the fall, and everybody from my home high school was counting on me to make it, because I was the only one who had been accepted. They said, "Sebastian, make us proud." They believed in me more than I believed in myself, and I came here and blew it away, and they were all so amazed.

Following graduation, Sebastian pursued a new summer opportunity. He interviewed and was hired as a counselor for a residential camp on campus for gifted and talented middle and high school students. Program participants engaged in fast-paced 3-week courses in areas of interest. Along with serving as a support staff member in the dormitory, Sebastian enjoyed helping to facilitate athletic competitions, talent shows, cookouts, dances, and social time for the students. He explained, "I was excited about working with students who were just like me, who are gifted, who are ahead of the game and cannot go on because their school is not allowing them to take certain courses." He believed the academy had prepared him well for his role: "I could really connect to many of the students in the summer program." When discussing his experiences during our interview, he highlighted what he believed had led to his selection for the position: "The people in charge thought I'd be a good person for the job. I think they saw that I hold myself to a certain standard of professionalism. For example, I wore a nice shirt and tie for the interview." He continued, "I guess what also appealed to them was that I'm such a positive person all the time. People can't seem to understand why I'm so happy. If they understood what I went through in life, then they'd understand why I'm so upbeat."

Undergraduate Life

Sebastian described himself as an undergraduate "man on the move" and joked about his intensity and drive. He tackled university life with high energy in all areas: a heavy load of honors-level courses and involvement in extracurricular activities, including the university marching band's color guard. He enjoyed the intellectual challenge of the honors courses and the opportunity to engage in independent study projects under the guidance of an Honors College professor, who served as his mentor. At the time of the interview, he was enrolled in an honors course in differential equations and was pursuing a project with his professor, Dr. Richardson. He described their work:

> The main topic is biomathematics, so we are looking at biological systems such as predator-prey and modeling them with differential equations. For example, you have a predator and a prey in a population, and based on how many predators you have, it affects the prey, and the differential equations show that. It's really neat how you can model that. . . . Dr. Richardson is an upper-level professor so it may be hard for him to bring it down to the students' level. He's really fast-paced, and I've had to adapt to his teaching style, but it's my favorite course. I have weekly meetings with him. I asked for these meetings because

> I want to make sure I'm progressing. I get stressed out about meeting his requirements and rising to his expectations. I always want to exceed my professors' expectations so they'll remember me.

Sebastian believed that Honors College courses were designed to provide an authentic learning experience for students. They could become deeply involved with the content rather than simply accelerating and covering more material. He intended to graduate from the university with an Honors College diploma. He explained, "I'm driven by goals. I don't see any sense in accepting less than I can do." At the time of the interviews, Sebastian had a 3.85 grade point average and believed that if he continued at this level, he would have the honors diploma.

He joined the university International Club, a group of students focused on developing campuswide programs to raise awareness of issues international students face and increase acceptance of multicultural populations at the university. As an Honors College student, he was also a member of the National Society of Collegiate Scholars, an academic honor society dedicated to community service projects on campus and in the local community. Of all of his extracurricular activities, however, he said that the time he spent with the university's color guard was most substantial. He began his involvement as a freshman and was excited about the upcoming year because he had recently auditioned for the role of squad captain and was selected. He described the process:

> I had to prove that I could write [a] routine. I had to write my original routine for two of the marching songs and then perform in front of the entire color guard. They critiqued me and submitted their critiques to the band director. He reviewed them, and then I was interviewed. The interview with the band director ended up being a laidback conversation. He wanted to know what my vision was.

He said he was "stoked" to get a head start on the season and looked forward "to a stronger line of people and techniques so we can tackle more challenging routines." The time commitment to the color guard was significant and included writing routines, practice time and rehearsals, and performing at halftime throughout the fall football season. Color guard members earned one course credit for "Marching Band Music," which Sebastian felt was insufficient for the amount of time invested; however, he maintained that being involved meant having many good friendships. He pointed out that this activity was a great outlet for creative expression: "I find myself spinning in my room, doing various dance moves that we've performed in previous years, and I have a strong connection to that." He continued, "But it's more about the people I've met who are fun-loving like me. It makes me feel welcome."

Sebastian's Reflections and Aspirations for the Future

As the interviews concluded, he reflected on his experiences and described his plans for the future. He knew early in his undergraduate life that graduate degrees were part of his plan. Torn between his passion for both mathematics and biological sciences, he knew he still had time to pursue his interests in the Honors College and determine his career path. He smiled and said, "I just dream about my future. I look forward to being hooded, being able to write those three letters, Ph.D., after my name. Dr. Sebastian Tucker, Professor." He chatted about his dream of teaching at a university, and, having never been on a plane, he aspired to traveling internationally. He explained that he wanted to experience the various cuisines of European countries, recognizing the significant influence of the culinary training from his grandmother. He acknowledged that he was in a good place in his life and was appreciative:

> Although I have had difficult obstacles to overcome, I'm just so amazed and blessed to be where I am today. I could have taken another path, allowed negative influences to consume me and just driven off into nothingness and been completely lost . . . I don't know what it was, but there was something inside me that said, "You are a blessed individual with great intellectual capacity. Pursue your dreams and fly."

He was determined to not allow his past to dictate his future:

> I've often thought about my childhood experiences being shaped by my father's alcoholism, and some days I think it

happened for the good. It actually pushed me to not want to live like that ever. That was pretty much a seed in itself. I think much of my motivation stems from that.

As he reflected on influential individuals in his life, he spoke of his mother and her undying love and support for him: "She's always been there for me, no matter what. I have always known that I am loved, and she showed it in different ways." He explained that he was grateful for all of the teachers who "pushed me, challenged me and believed in me," including all of the teachers who knew what he was going through at home and supported him emotionally and encouraged him to excel. He also described the academy's director as the "best person ever," because he facilitated thought-provoking seminars with Sebastian's senior class that helped him gain insights about himself. Sebastian explained, "He taught sessions on how to find yourself, being true to yourself, how to build relationships, what is important to you in life. They were such deep topics that we discussed for hours, but he really hit home with me." He concluded with memories from his childhood and thoughts of his beloved grandmother:

> I would say that my grandmother really made a difference for me. I remember numerous times coming home from church, and I knew that we were getting ready to walk into a house of hell. She would sit in the car and talk to us for about 15 or 20 minutes before we had to go in, and she would tell us, "I stress to you that your education is your way out. You get that education and you won't ever have to deal with this again." She just kept telling me that, and it was simply ingrained in my head.

Epilogue

Sebastian Tucker graduated from the Honors College at the university. He was awarded a predoctoral fellowship from the National Health Institute and earned a master's degree in cell and molecular biology from a state university on the West Coast. He is currently a Ph.D. candidate in the Department of Cell and Developmental Biology at a prestigious Midwestern university medical school.

CHAPTER 5

PATRICK

Patrick Brennan was seated at a table by the window in the coffee shop when I entered. He greeted me with a firm handshake and a warm, friendly smile. With his rugged athletic physique and his classic khakis and a freshly starched plaid sport shirt, he reminded me of a model in a sporty men's clothing catalog. After ordering our coffee, Patrick and I proceeded to a quiet conference room in the coffee shop where we were guaranteed to have private conversation. Exchanging pleasantries took little time, and I soon realized that my work with this gentleman would be relaxed. Patrick had an easygoing manner and was a natural conversationalist. As we began the initial interview, he explained that he had brought helpful props with him. He shared a collection of 5" x 7" index cards with key points in his life story that he wanted to share. These cards were not new. Patrick had earlier been invited to share his story with a number of professional groups with a presentation entitled, "From Dummy to Doctor." The cards were reminders of the significant points he wanted to be sure he would address. He joked about his use of cue cards, and I assured him I'd discuss those key points carefully with him. Impressed with his sincerity and his determination to be thorough in sharing his experiences, I knew immediately that this journey with Patrick would be enjoyable. Our laughs began with the cards and continued throughout our work together.

Patrick's story is that of a highly intelligent young man with a history of learning difficulties. In his mid-30s, he had recently earned his doctoral degree in educational leadership from a major research university and was employed as an educational consultant.

The Brennan Family

Patrick was the youngest child in an Irish Catholic family of five boys and one girl. Born in a quiet suburban New England community, he explained that his parents initially lived in "Rainbow Terrace," a subsidized housing community, a benefit of his father's earlier military service. Eventually they purchased a "summer camp type of home" and expanded the house as they raised their family. His father was employed as a lineman for New England Telephone, and his mother remained home caring for her family. Patrick explained, "We grew up in the community as it was becoming the affluent coastal suburb that it is today." He described this context as a "blessing and a curse because in that community everybody goes to college." His parents "were all about education and doing better than they had done." As a first-generation college student, Patrick recognized the sacrifices his parents had made for their children. He described their challenges:

> My dad was a really frustrated guy. He was real tough, hardcore alcoholic, kind of abusive, but a good person. He was a good guy, and all he did was work for us. He constantly worked overtime. He did everything for his kids. He provided, but he had a hard time showing his love in a nurturing way. He was a good man, but a troubled man. . . . A guy with a huge temper and scream, and you could get hit with a belt. . . . He wasn't educated but he was a flippin' genius. He was rather frustrated and he had a chip on his shoulder. Dad was a prolific reader. You'd ask him anything, and he would know it.

Patrick saw that his father's experiences in school were similar to his. He indicated that his father seldom talked about his own schooling; however, when he did, he highlighted being a voracious reader but never performing well on tests.

Patrick's maternal grandfather died when his mother was only 4, and his grandmother kept the family together "scrubbing floors and getting the job done for her kids." Mrs. Brennan had graduated from high school and did some secretarial work. She was a strong source of support for Patrick, and sadly, he lost her to cancer a month before his college graduation. He explained, "My dissertation was dedicated to her because without her, I wouldn't be in [this shop] today talking to you about this." His father lived a decade beyond his mother's death. Patrick explained:

> He lived the life of Reilly [an enviable life]. He had a girlfriend, and they spent summers in coastal New England and winters in Key Largo, FL. He did quite well, but he was a man of excess. He ate too much and drank too much and smoked too much, and eventually, he had an aortic aneurism. He went out in a blaze of glory.

Patrick's reflections of his childhood included stories of an action-packed household, big meals, family get-togethers, and good times with his siblings. His brothers and sister provided him with a broad variety of success models throughout his adolescence. Patrick's oldest brother, John, was 14 years older than he was. Patrick referred to John as the "superstar of the family" and explained that he and his siblings really admired their oldest brother. In high school, John was an all-American athlete and a top-notch scholar who eventually graduated from Dartmouth University and went on to become a financial analyst on Wall Street. Patrick's sister, Jane, had difficulty throughout adolescence as a lesbian growing up in an Irish Catholic family; however, following a long search for identity, she earned a master's degree and became a teacher working with children with severe behavior problems. The third child, Peter, graduated from Villanova University where he was student body president and later earned an MBA. Patrick chuckled as he described Peter and explained his area of expertise in medical business: "He's the suit guy behind doctors." Ted was 6 years older than Patrick and the one older brother who struggled in school. He faced learning difficulties, survived high school, and entered the Navy, where his technical orientation aligned with his assignment as a radioman involved in military intelligence. He completed his tour of duty, earned a college degree while working full-time, and eventually was successful in corporate sales. Patrick smiled as he said, "He makes a ton of money, but he's a fun guy to know because his priority in life is to enjoy himself. He finds the space in the world to be happy in." Timmy, a popular athlete with a constant bevy of girlfriends, was the brother closest in age to Patrick. Timmy did not take academics seriously and was able to coast through his school years with minimal effort. He graduated from the state's maritime academy and served in the Merchant Marines. He earned a master's degree in engineering and at the time of the interview, he was supervising the physical plant of a large private college in New England.

Although Patrick was proud of all of his siblings, he acknowledged that his emotional bonds with Ted and Timmy, the brothers closest in age to him, remained the strongest. He pointed out that they phoned or texted one another daily, and they were the two cheerleaders who checked in with him as he wrote his doctoral dissertation, always asking "How's the book report coming?"

Early Years in School

Patrick described his mother's important role in the education of her children. Having closely observed the development of his five older siblings, she found Patrick to be verbal and articulate, giving her no reason to assume he would have problems in school. Patrick chuckled as he explained the "Margaret Mary Brennan Catalog-Based Intelligence Test." His mother would place her children in her lap with a store catalog and point to items on the pages and have them "talk about the balls and the sports equipment and the household appliances." Patrick explained:

> Years later she told me, "I knew you were as smart as your brother at Dartmouth." She was intrigued that I could name so many things in the book at a very young age. She thought I was bright, and you can take her word for it, because she raised six kids, so she was quite an expert!

Patrick reflected on his preschool years and pointed out that his family may have overlooked several critical indicators of potential learning difficulties. "There were some hand dominance issues going on." He explained, "I had a really hard time tying my shoes, and sports became a real problem because in baseball I was throwing the ball with both hands." He confessed that he also could not hit the ball. He remembered that cutting with scissors was also impossible for him. He reflected on these early years:

> I am by no means an expert in this area, and these issues may not be a telltale sign of problems, but neurodevelopment people say that you should take pause when you see things like this because it's an indicator that something might be a little off when kids are having some problems with motor skills. It would be something worth looking into.

His earliest memories of school were painful. "I hated school early on. I remember having headaches in kindergarten, and I remember worrying about getting headaches, and I also remember about lying about them in order to stay home from school." His situation grew worse in first grade:

> I couldn't learn math facts and I couldn't learn to tell time. Organizationally, I was the kid with the lost papers stuffed in my pockets that came out in the wash. If I had any strengths, they were in language. I could write well, and I was verbal, but because of all the problems I was having, I was in the low reading group—the blue birds group.
>
> I was a blue bird, and I knew it. Here in the South, I would have been in the Bless Their Hearts group.

Patrick underwent testing by the school psychologist in first grade and was diagnosed with a learning disability. "I got the formal diagnosis as LD, and the resource room came into play. The resource room was where children like I were sent away while everyone else went on with their lives." Reflecting on his experience in the resource room, he called attention to how his time spent in the resource room had an impact on his not being exposed to content in the regular classroom:

> I worked with an occupational therapist on reading and writing, but I was missing out on content. When I took the first battery of standardized tests, I remember leaving the resource room and coming into the mainstream environment with the rows of desks, and everything had been taken off the walls. I looked at that booklet. I literally did not read it. I just Christmas treed. So it was now another reason to bless my heart. "Oh look, he's slow, he doesn't know anything, and now [he's] Christmas treeing things."

Patrick's developmental challenges with learning influenced his life beyond the classroom, and his anxiety increased. He played on a football team and struggled to understand what was going on. "I had a difficult time understanding the game. If you want to really hit my weakness, it's x's and o's and circles left and right, and who goes where. I didn't get it, and I had a coach who would yell, scream, and would call you a cream puff if you didn't understand." His challenges also influenced his life on the school playground, and he admitted that he began to hate recess. The Rubik's Cube craze arrived, and his friends were engrossed in solving the puzzle, but Patrick found that he could not tackle such a spatial task. Mad Libs proved to be another source of frustration because he had not been exposed to the language arts content necessary to achieve success. "So even in games that pulled from mainstream content, I didn't even have a chance. I just felt dumb."

His self-esteem did not improve when he took on delivering newspapers in his neighborhood. With a paper route of 24 papers to be delivered, Patrick inevitably arrived home with two or three newspapers remaining, and his mother would say, "But we counted them?" Shortly after, the Brennans received phone calls from angry customers who had not received their papers. When it came time to collect payment and maintain records, Patrick's lack of organizational skills exacerbated the situation. This evolved into more interaction with angry adults and increasing anxiety for the paperboy. He explained, "So school, sports, recess, and even little jobs . . . I was starting to think, 'I really can't do anything.'"

Patrick provided an analysis of his situation and labeled it "chronic success deprivation." He explained, "It was the perfect storm. I have the LD label, I'm in the resource room, there's no content, I have low achievement scores, anxiety is increasing, self-esteem is going down, and I'm developing this learned helplessness." He continued, "I'm sure I was beginning to throw the towel in a bit. I'm being perceived as lazy, and my anxiety is getting really bad."

By third grade, Patrick's father intervened with his tough love approach to the problem. Thinking that his son was lazy, he grounded Patrick in the summer, insisting that he learn his multiplication tables. He sent him to his bedroom with a yellow legal pad with the multiplication tables written out. Patrick spent hours alone in his room in tears. Eventually his father acquiesced when he found his son in a heap of tears and crinkled yellow paper and realized that his son really wanted to know his multiplication facts and was not being obstinate.

Dad's tough love did not work, nor did the efforts of the resource room teacher. Referring to her as "Mrs. Crabapple," Patrick indicated that she became a villain in his experiences, as she would publicly humiliate him in front of his friends:

> There was this sweet little girl from New Zealand who I had a crush on. I have a vivid memory of standing in line to get my chocolate milk. I remember having my milk ticket, and along came Mrs. Crabapple, who started asking me multiplication facts in front of this girl. I just remember the anxiety, the heat in my face, and my heart pounding.

These physiological responses increased. Patrick experienced heart palpitations, more headaches, and overwhelming feelings of anxiety, all of which led him to shut down whenever asked to perform.

In fourth grade, an annual IEP meeting was held, and the group of educators around the conference table proposed to Patrick's parents that he repeat fourth grade. Refusing to accept this proposal, Mrs. Brennan discovered that Children's Hospital Boston was collaborating with Harvard University and facilitating batteries of testing done by a noted pediatric researcher and a team of research associates. She succeeded in getting Patrick registered for the evaluation and planned for several days of testing. He smiled as he reflected on his overnight excursion into the city: "I remember eating Chinese food and going to Boston Commons and riding the swan boats. It was a good deal." He also shared vivid memories of the intelligence testing: "I remember red blocks, and timed watches, and being asked to do motor stuff. I remember being intensely tired." More importantly, he shared a poignant memory of the conclusion of the experience. "The doctor knelt down in front of me and said, 'Don't you ever forget that you are a very smart little boy. Don't you ever let anyone tell you that you aren't smart.'"

Patrick's mother returned to the school district armed with records of the assessment. The pediatric research team discovered that Patrick's situation could be explained by developmental delays. His profile was that of a young boy who was quite verbal and who struggled with spatial abilities. The testing indicated that his generalized knowledge placed him in the 99th percentile. He had learned a great deal from his father reading the newspaper to him, from watching *Wild, Wild World of Animals*, from playing vocabulary games with his brothers, and from exploring globes and maps of the world with his father. The assessment indicated that Patrick needed exposure to more content, accommodations for eye-hand coordination, and audio strategies, oral exams, and extended time on tests.

Returning home from Boston, Mrs. Brennan believed that she could make life better for Patrick. Having learned of several neighborhood friends who were enrolling their children in St. Dominic's Elementary, a parochial school in a neighboring community, she decided to investigate this possibility for her son. He explained, "I think my mother thought that if special education can't save him, maybe God will." Mrs. Brennan met with the nuns at St. Dominic's, and they explained that they were not equipped to accommodate students with learning disabilities. Patrick smiled as he described the scenario: "We'll pray for him, but we can't take him." His mother was hoping that a change of school would provide him with a fresh start. She had no choice but to return to the public school armed with the new IEP from the pediatric research team. She worked with her son as he dictated his responses to assignments and she typed. The school did not respond favorably to this approach. The administration paid no attention to the IEP provided by the pediatric researcher and his colleagues. Patrick's father was furious with the school district because he had invested a substantial amount of money on Patrick's assessment at Children's Hospital only to have school administrators dismiss it. Patrick recalled that his dad insisted on helping him build a windmill as a science fair project. He explained, "Truth be told, my dad did the whole thing. He went psycho! He was so psyched! He built the entire thing from popsicle sticks." Patrick received a grade of C on the project, and his father swore it was rigged against him. "My dad knew it was over for me. From then on, he advised me to be nice. Nice gets you a long way."

By fifth grade, Patrick's frustration with his situation led him to explore a different set of friends. A group of boys who lived on Dodge Road in the community were known for being problems in school. Patrick became intrigued with the Dodge Road kids and spent time in the woods at their "fort" smoking cigarettes, chewing tobacco, drinking beer, and investigating *Playboy* magazine. When his older brother Ted learned of this, Ted was concerned, for he knew the older brothers of these young men and warned Patrick that his new chosen crowd would one day be the "druggies." Ted's advice was, "Get out of Dodge!" Fortunately, Patrick listened to Ted.

The Middle School Years

Sixth, seventh, and eighth grades were difficult years for Patrick. He was highly anxious and suffered from migraine headaches and nausea from the stress of school. One of his worst memories was of a seventh-grade language arts class, which was created for a group of students receiving resource room support. Patrick's theory was that the school staff was attempting to create a "mainstream environment to make us feel like we were going to a real English class." The students and their teacher met in a room that had previously been a custodial closet. With no window, and a few small desks and chalkboard filling the room, the teacher was forced to keep the classroom door open. Patrick remembered his strategy for avoiding "public humiliation" by waiting until all of his friends had arrived at their classrooms before he walked to the closet. "I remember I was there with eight kids in the janitor's closet! It was devastating."

His memories also included being mainstreamed into a social science class in which the teacher required that students maintain an organized 3-ring binder. Notebook checks were part of the teacher's assessment. Patrick smiled as he explained, "All he cared about was that damn notebook, and I simply couldn't do it. I could not stay organized." He asked, "Tell me, what standards are we addressing for organizing a notebook in social studies?"

Throughout his middle school years, Patrick had visions of attending St. Joseph's Preparatory High School. His older brothers had all attended St. Joseph's. Like his oldest brother John, the population of students attending this Catholic prep school typically went on to study at Boston College, Dartmouth College, and Harvard University. Patrick's family had been immersed in the culture of St. Joseph's his entire life, with his parents devoting a great deal of time to fundraising events for the school. Patrick reported that even Brother Keith, the headmaster, had said, "You'll soon be here one day." When Patrick shared these plans with his teachers at the middle school, they were polite and did not discourage him.

Patrick vividly described to me the IEP meeting that occurred in eighth grade. A group of teachers and administrators came together to meet with Patrick and his mother to plan for high school. He described it in detail:

> "Mrs. Brennan we need to talk about next year." They laid it out there. "Patrick is not one of the brightest bulbs in the chandelier. There is a bleak future ahead. Let's get real, Mrs. Brennan." The gist of the conversation was "Patrick will be able to swing a hammer or pick up trash." It was really that sinister, and in the middle of the conversation, my mother grabbed me by the hand and walked out. We got into the car, and I thought we were going to get ice cream and go home. Instead, she drove to a neighboring community, and we pulled into St. Dominic's parking lot. My mother grabs me by the wrist, drags me with her and knocks on the front door of the school. Sister Alice appears and my mother says, "Can I have a moment of your time, Sister Alice?" We went into her office, and my mother said, "Do you remember me from several years ago when I wanted my son in this school and you denied him? I just walked out of my son's middle school, I pulled him out, and he's not going back. If you don't accept him, I'm going to jail because he is not going back." I was in a Catholic school uniform the next day. That's what it takes. You need a mother who's willing to beat up a nun for you.

Life at St. Dominic's

Patrick was accepted at St. Dominic's for a month-long probationary period. Arriving with his new school uniform, he found himself facing tremendous challenges. Not having been exposed to the content he needed, the eighth-grade curriculum proved to be daunting. When he arrived in English class, students were handling advanced grammar. He explained,

> I can't do Mad Libs, and they're diagramming sentences! I hadn't been in a real math class, and they were doing prealgebra. I didn't know my own language, and they had a

French class! Music for me had been shaking a tambourine, and they're playing recorders and reading music.

He was overwhelmed by the assigned homework and claimed he could not do it. He remembered severe migraine headaches, sitting in class twitching nervously, and escaping to the restroom to vomit. At the end of his probationary period, Sister Alice met with Patrick and his mother. The conversation in the principal's office centered on Patrick's lack of success in this new environment and the school's decision to dismiss him. Mrs. Brennan refused to accept this and insisted that Patrick was not leaving. He smiled as he reported, "I've been here for a month, and my mom is going to beat up a nun again!" Sister Alice then proposed that Patrick be dropped back to seventh grade, and his mother agreed. He described how he felt the following morning as he transitioned back to seventh grade:

> We're driving to school. I'm crying and pleading with my mother. "Please, please don't make me do this." This wasn't getting held back, this wasn't retention, this was public humiliation. I could hear the drumbeat as I was walking up to the gallows. I had to get my stuff out of the eighth-grade wing and walk into the seventh-grade classroom. Kids asked, "Weren't you in eighth grade?" I responded with "I didn't like eighth-grade girls so I thought I'd try seventh!" It was so humiliating.

Patrick explained that he had reflected on this experience as an adult and had learned to be proud of his resilience during this period. He admitted that he had such strong doubts about his abilities and experienced suicidal thoughts, but somehow managed to find the internal fortitude to survive that academic year.

With the shift to seventh grade, several positive things happened for Patrick. Shortly before leaving his public middle school midyear, he had been voted "Best Looking Eighth-Grade Boy" as part of the School Superlatives in the class yearbook. When he transitioned to seventh grade at St. Dominic's, the seventh-grade girls were happy he was joining them. Recognized as a handsome teenager, he found he was invited to class parties and was welcomed by the students. His social capital also increased greatly when he emerged as the fastest runner in seventh grade. His physical education teacher incorporated competitive races, and Patrick excelled. Having grown up playing football with many older brothers, he was well trained as a runner. He became known as the fastest kid at St. Dominic's, and he stood out among his peers at recess and in gym class. In addition, Sister Alice, the school principal, did her best to support him. She called him to her office one afternoon and explained that she had purchased a very expensive camera for the school and was selecting him to serve as the school's official photographer. She handed him the expensive camera, told him to go home and read the instruction manual, practice taking pictures, and then she would expect him to shoot photographs of important events throughout the school year. Patrick reflected, "She must have seen some aptitude in me and noted that I could handle a social setting. It was the first time in my life that somebody ever acknowledged that I could do something. I was in charge of the school camera. That was pretty darn cool."

He found that teachers were supportive. Both the nuns and the lay teachers were "sweet ladies who were loving but firm." He respected them. Eventually his situation began to improve academically. He was making significant leaps in skill development in language arts and reading and found success with oral presentations. His strengths began to emerge, and the faculty recognized and celebrated this improvement. He admitted, "I wish I could tell you that the clouds opened up and my academic struggles disappeared, but that wasn't the case." He acknowledged he had compassionate teachers in his French and math classes and pointed out that the school's lack of ability grouping enabled him not to feel stigmatized.

Patrick described his culminating achievement at St. Dominic's as one that had his parents and siblings in total disbelief. He was selected to lead the eighth-grade graduation procession of students into the church as he carried the crucifix. He explained, "This was typically an honor that was reserved for the best and brightest student in the class. So, for whatever reason, they saw something in me and wanted me to represent the class." He elaborated, "My parents said it was a wonderful thing. It was good for me, my claim to fame. It told us those people were nice, they were acknowledging my effort. They saw I worked hard and never gave up."

High School Years at St. Joseph's Prep

With four older brothers who were alumni of St. Joseph's Preparatory High School, Patrick explained, "We were what they called a prep family. I grew up there; we were there all the time. The brothers who taught there knew me personally." Patrick's eldest brother, John, had been one of the top academic students, an all-star athlete, and honored as "Mr. St. Joseph's Prep" in his senior year. His brother Peter also had a stellar record and had served as class president and star athlete. It was understood that the Brennan's family legacy would influence Patrick's admission to the school. Patrick understood that the reputations of his older brothers would be a challenge for him. He explained that, throughout the summer, he began to have "internal whisperings." He found himself thinking, "This isn't legit. I'm not as smart as my brothers. I'm not smart enough to do this. This is going to be ugly." Patrick took the entrance exam, and the family waited for the admissions acceptance letter to arrive. Shortly after the letter appeared in the mail, Patrick pointed out that "reality hit" when the school's summer reading list soon followed. Patrick felt panic. Although dyslexia was not part of his learning profile, he had managed to get through school without ever having read an entire book. He noted, "There were several Tolkien books! *Robinson Crusoe* was on the list. I started to read some, I rented movies, I even bought Monarch notes." He described how this approach did not work for him: "I go to English class. Day One. Welcome to St. Joseph's. Clear your desks please. Take out a piece of paper and a pencil. She had a quiz on all the reading! So it was failure from day one."

As a middle school student, Patrick had been recognized as a fast runner. By the time he arrived at St. Joseph's, he had developed into a very fast runner. Although he did not pay enough attention to the summer reading list, he dedicated much of his time to lifting weights and sprinting. He had decided to try out for the St. Joseph's football team. He explained, "Because football was such a big thing for my family, and I had given it a go as a kid and I had difficulty with it conceptually, I thought I would redeem myself in the eyes of my father and my family." When football tryouts were held, Patrick discovered that he was the fastest runner. He reported that during tryouts, he scored a 4.7 in a 40-yard dash! When the freshman squad team roster was publicly announced in the gymnasium, Patrick's name was called first. He indicated, "So while I'm getting punched in the face with the summer reading list and struggling academically, something good happened to me, and that was significant."

Patrick had long received messages from his mother about the importance of being polite and pleasant. Those lessons were important, and Patrick's practical intelligence emerged as he decided to address his academic challenges with his teachers. He described his approach:

> I knew that I was really falling behind. I decided that when the final bell would ring at the end of the day, I would make the rounds. I would go to every teacher after school just to meet with them. "I don't understand this, could you please explain this to me again? "Is there something I could do for extra credit?" Some days it was simply to drop in and say "Hi! How are you doing?" I did this to reconnect with them, establish a relationship, develop a rapport, and let them know that I cared.

Patrick indicated that these visits with teachers after school were important in that he came to know which teachers understood his situation. He realized that he had developed an ability to read people well. He explained that living with an alcoholic father whose moods needed to be read daily prepared him to "navigate teachers" and their expectations for him.

During his freshman year, Patrick discovered Sister Anne, a nun who directed the campus ministry office and enjoyed having students visit. There, he found a refuge from the challenges he faced in school. He explained, "I would swing by there periodically. She was nice. There were comfortable chairs, and you could enjoy snacks. She was there to listen, and she provided an environment that was calm. It was a pleasant place to be."

As Patrick struggled academically and attempted to maintain positive relationships with his teachers, he faced serious challenges on the football field. When he arrived for the first day of practice, he was handed a 3-ring binder with all of the team's plays in it. He explained, "It was really like having another academic class. You were supposed to take that book home and memorize the plays." He indicated that he was so busy attempting to keep up with his daily homework that he didn't have time to be looking at football plays. He explained,

> If you did an analysis of my learning profile and what goes on in a football game, it doesn't match up very well conceptually. The 3-ring binder filled with circles and arrows, the problems with my processing speed, and then add the coaches yelling at you. And my dad would come to practice every day and watch from the fence, and at the end of the day, I would get yelled at again. I started to experience high anxiety.

The football coaches were not faculty members with training in adolescent development, but community members hired by the school to serve in this part-time role. As Patrick explained, "The coaches thought I was an idiot. If someone had understood me and was passionate about teaching, and remained calm and could have broken it down, I could have learned it, but I was so panicked."

He smiled when he explained that he owns a sign that reads, "Damn you Forrest Gump!" As one who appreciated the classic movie starring Tom Hanks, Patrick identified with that movie's hero. "If I could just run, I would run fast. I could get around. I could score touchdowns.

Eventually, the coaches developed a plan that enabled Patrick to succeed. "We developed two plays, sweep left and sweep right. The quarterback pitches the ball to Patrick and everybody runs left and he runs behind and runs for daylight. Sweep right, we pitch the ball to Patrick and everybody runs right." He chuckled as he explained, "I scored touchdowns all the time. I could run, and I had the instinct to get around people. Anything improvisational was great, if I didn't have an assignment. I could just run with the ball."

As Patrick was recognized for his athletic success, he realized he needed to maintain what he referred to as "the 70% plan." A passing grade at St. Joseph's was 70. Any grades below that prohibited students from participating in sports and extracurricular activities. Patrick reflected, "If you look at my report cards from that time, I wasn't doing well. I was failing classes. On the report card there was an amazing mathematical coincidence occurring. My biology class may have been a 79 or 80, but everything else was 70." Patrick theorized, "Teachers were saying 'He's a good kid. I'm going to throw him a bone.' I was a nice kid, and for me, sometimes the rules were bent, policies were shifted, and curriculum was forsaken, so I remained eligible for sports on the 70% plan."

As part of his football regimen, Patrick found that he really enjoyed the wind sprints that were a requirement of daily practices. Although most members of the team hated them, Patrick realized that he enjoyed something that he excelled in: "It didn't take much effort. I didn't have to think about it. The whistle blows and you just run. I blew everyone away, and the coaches noticed." As a result, the coaches suggested that he consider going out for the winter track team. When Patrick tried out for the team, it was readily apparent that he was the fastest runner there. He earned a place on the varsity team as a freshman. In that group, Patrick met athletes who were "funkier kids, a bit more scholarly, a little more nerdy, but nice." The track team's coach was Rob Casey, a history teacher that Patrick "really just clicked with," a man known for his intensity. On the first day of track practice, Patrick discovered he was lactic acid intolerant and became violently ill from running. He described a significant moment with his new coach:

> I remember vomiting and he walked up to me and put his arm around me, and he said. "Come on, you can do one more. You can do one more. You can do it again." I remember being stunned, but I was thrilled with the intensity of just sucking it up. Your legs are on fire, you're throwing up, but you just do it again anyway. He would say that, "Just do it again!" That became kind of sick and twisted, but I was attracted to that. "This hurts, but I really love it." He was intense, and I found I was intense and willing to push through the pain. I think that's what he liked in kids—kids with drive who could suck it up and dig. So we hit it off pretty well.

On the track team, Patrick was successful, winning numerous races throughout the season and earning a title in the 50-yard dash in a statewide conference. He explained that he "enjoyed getting lots of ink in the local newspaper's sports page, not having to worry about looking bad in front of my peers, and my coach loved me." He pointed out that he survived his freshman year on the 70% plan and was identified in St. Joseph's school newspaper as "Super Frosh" for the splash he had made on the varsity level track team. As his freshman year came to an end, Patrick experienced another "kick in the teeth" when he learned that he had failed algebra and would have to attend summer school to recoup his grade. Instead, Patrick's mother hired a math tutor who worked through extensive algebra workbooks with him. These daily sessions resulted in the tutor documenting the work he had completed in order for St.

Joseph's to grant him the algebra credit. Although Patrick was relieved that his classmates never learned that he had failed algebra, he explained the work with the tutor certainly "ruined a summer."

The Full Casey Treatment

Returning to St. Joseph's for his sophomore year, Patrick struggled with whether to play football. Admitting that he did not want to play, he confessed, "I did it for my dad. He was so excited about it." But the season proved to be excruciating. When serving on the junior varsity team, he maintained his tradition of scoring touchdowns with the team's right- and left-sweep strategy; however, he was sent into varsity games when the quarterback would call out an amendment in the play, and Patrick would panic on the field.

Sophomore year was torture for Patrick academically. With a schedule that included Spanish, geometry, and chemistry, three classes that exposed his weaknesses, he was overwhelmed. He negotiated a switch to another Spanish class where he connected with a teacher whom he described as a "genuine nice guy" who loved Bob Dylan and enjoyed talking with Patrick about music. He appreciated Patrick's learning profile and provided him tutorial sessions after school and the opportunity to retake quizzes. He maintained the 70% plan in his other classes, but the stress and frustration coupled with anxiety led to bouts of depression. "There would be days when I would arrive home from school, and I'd be in my bedroom just sobbing. My parents didn't know what to do. I had serious thoughts of dropping out of high school. It was really that bad." Patrick shared his frustrations with the guidance counselor assigned to him and later learned that was a mistake. He discovered from Coach Casey that his guidance counselor was using confidential information with other teachers in the faculty lounge in an attempt to convince them that Patrick was not "St. Joseph's Prep material." Patrick reflected on a profound conversation with his coach in the school corridor. In that discussion, Rob Casey took Patrick on as his protégé and insisted, "You got a problem, you come to me. I'm your coach, I'm your guidance counselor now unofficially, and next semester, I'm teaching history and you'll be in my class, too." That year, Patrick realized that he had earned the "Full Casey Treatment"—a genuine mentor who would continue to support him in multiple ways during the remainder of his schooling at St. Joseph's.

Coach Casey arranged to have Patrick assigned to a new guidance counselor, a woman who spent time thoughtfully reviewing his situation. Together, the counselor and Rob Casey convinced Patrick that it was in his best interests to repeat Algebra I again as a junior. Knowing that he would encounter the SATs and a major part of the math section was algebra, they were convinced that if he had mastery of freshman algebra, he would survive. Patrick described this as another round of public humiliation. "At this point I'm older. I'm shaving! High school freshmen are babies. It was brutal." Fortunately, the algebra teacher was an assistant track coach who assured Patrick that by working together in algebra, they "could get the job done." Although he realized it would be embarrassing, he agreed to the plan.

During the summer after his sophomore year, Patrick was employed as a stock boy and spent time with the other employees listening to classic rock on the radio as they worked. He and his colleagues entertained themselves with competitions in naming the songs featured and the associated artists. He explained that he became known for his aptitude for learning names of songs and artists. "I could name the song after one note had been played. It was a rather insignificant thing, but for the first time in my life, I was competing in a cognitive game where people were testing their brains, going man-to-man." That same summer Patrick enjoyed a relationship with his first girlfriend, Susan Perkins, a young woman from a neighboring community who excelled academically. While spending time with her, he found he reflected back on his sophomore year and began to think about the aptitude and strengths he had and how he might have applied them differently. He decided to focus on the things he could do well and use his strength areas to meet success. As a result of this self-reflection, he made a personal pledge to earn a place on the headmaster's list at St. Joseph's the next academic year. He saw Susan as "bound for Georgetown" and needed to know how she managed her academic routine. "I didn't want her to tutor me. I simply needed her organizational strategies." He described Susan's approach to school: "We went downtown and bought all the loose leaf binders and paper we needed, and I implemented her system—a hole punch in each notebook so when the teacher gives you a handout, you date it, punch it in, and keep it in sequential order. I never lost papers again!" Realizing

110

that success in his junior year would be critical if he had any intentions of attending college, he seriously read the books on St. Joseph's summer reading list, worked out in the gym, and vowed that the upcoming year would be a turning point.

Junior Year—The Full Casey Treatment Continues

In his junior year, Patrick decided not to play football. Although he might have disappointed his father, he knew he excelled in running and enjoyed track, and his focus had to be on academics. He maintained his strategy of meeting with all of his teachers after school and spent the fall semester hanging out with Coach Casey and the cross-country team in order to prepare for track in the spring. With the support of his guidance counselor, he enrolled in classes that were aligned with his learning profile. Chemistry was replaced with geology, a course students referred to as "Rocks for Jocks;" however, Patrick realized it suited his needs. "There were no formulas, no grams to moles and moles to grams." Having completed his foreign language requirements, he enrolled in U.S. History, Algebra I, English, and biology. With his modified curriculum, his newfound organizational system, his desire to do well, and no daily football practice, he succeeded in making the headmaster's list with grades of 85 or better in every class. His mother was elated, and his father was genuinely proud. He continued to excel in track and was named to the state's All Star team.

During his junior year, Patrick's mother arranged for him to complete a second battery of tests that helped to certify his learning disability. This strategic move was critical, because documentation of the disability would enable him to complete the SAT's in an untimed fashion. With this accommodation in place, his stress level was much lower and he scored 1020. "It was unbelievable. The next day I took the letter to the headmaster and to my coach, and they were so elated." Patrick smiled as he reflected on the "Margaret Mary Brennan Catalog-Based Intelligence Test" and explained that his mother responded to the news with "See, I knew this about you. I told you this." He also indicated that his father was "genuinely proud" and wrote letters to extended family members about this great news. He summarized, "So my junior year went really well. I earned B's and high B's. I'm an All-Star in athletics, and I break 1000 on the SATs. I was able to hold my head a little higher."

During the summer following his junior year, Patrick continued to benefit from the Full Casey Treatment. His coach offered him a summer job at his family-owned restaurant, "Casey's Roast Beef"—a popular seaside establishment with a long history of serving sandwiches and seafood. Patrick's job involved taking orders at one of the 14 service windows. The pace of business was extremely fast, and Patrick struggled to maintain his composure. He faced total frustration as he tried to make change and remember the beverages and the condiments the customers ordered, and he struggled furiously as he was expected to complete the order in 3 to 5 minutes without writing it down. He remembered the angry looks of the customers' faces and described how this experience brought on serious panic attacks. His memories of these attacks were vivid:

> You're asked to do something, and suddenly you get so focused on that task and people judging you or it being revealed that you can't do something or that you're stupid or a fraud, and you are so consumed with thinking about all of those things that you're not thinking of the task at hand. What happens is a flush of heat and sweating, heart palpitations and a feeling like you're about to fall over and pass out. It's out of proportion, and you know it. It's a roast beef sandwich; it doesn't warrant this response. But in the moment you can't get out of it, and it reaches the point where you can't talk or you can't breathe. You're sweaty, and you have to rush to the bathroom.

The first time this occurred, Patrick escaped to the men's room and managed to pull himself together; however, his view of himself was shaken as he watched other employees who were high school dropouts handle the job effortlessly. He explained his feelings:

> A huge part of my learning barrier was this emotional component, the self-doubt. I'd be thinking, "I'm a dummy." You simply can't learn like that. I couldn't even learn to make roast beef sandwiches, but meanwhile I was on the honor roll at St. Joseph's Prep. It just didn't make sense.

Patrick reflected on this experience at the restaurant to his academic life. "Just as I start to do well, there's always something that happens to me.

The impostor syndrome kicks in, which keeps you humble—'Hmmm, maybe you're no so bright.'" Eventually Patrick gained control of his situation and managed to develop strategies to survive the hectic quality of the work. The job paid well, and he maintained it through high school. The opportunity to work at the restaurant represented the thoroughness of the Full Casey Treatment he received, and he realized that his coach was certainly investing a great deal of personal energy in Patrick's school experience and personal development. Patrick highlighted how grateful he was for his mentor's approach and explained how he committed himself to the man:

> Casey gave me the metaphor. He described in graphic detail the perspective of a successful runner. He would talk about the feelings of pain and perseverance. He'd say, "What you do in our track practice, gentlemen, is step to the line. And you run and you run." If you said, "No, I'm quitting," he'd say, "You can step to the line right now, you can step to the line at a track meet, you can step to the line in your classes, you can step to the line when you're going to ask someone to marry you. You step to the line when you ask for a promotion. You step to the line when you do the right thing." He talked about those times when it was about sucking it up and just doing it anyway. And that would happen, because there were many times I'd be nervous before a class or a test, and I'd just go step to the line. I wrote him a letter many years after I left St. Joseph's. I wrote, "Though I haven't donned a track uniform in a long time, I still step to the line every day."

Senior Year and the College Search

Patrick continued to enjoy academic success in his senior year in high school. He pointed out that he had survived the embarrassment of taking Algebra I a second time and had earned a grade of 80. From then on, his high school transcript was a portrait of A's and high B's, which resulted in his not having to take final exams in many of his courses. He explained that he realized, "I'm not stupid, and not only am I at St. Joseph's, but I'm performing. It took 2 years to get there, but I had 2 years of success in the end." When the college application process began early in his senior year, he crafted his essay, carefully highlighting the success he had achieved during his junior year. He summarized his essay with, "I'm diagnosed as LD, and I've been a mess, but please look at my junior year. Just look at it again and know that I'm going to do that again senior year, and I plan to continue this progress in college."

Patrick's success in his senior year also included his receiving an important accolade. The faculty at St. Joseph's awarded him the "Gold Award" in religion. He explained that his theology classes were not about memorizing and regurgitating but involved critical thinking and debate, which were aligned with his academic strengths. Having spent time with Sister Anne in the campus ministry office discussing theological issues, Patrick assumed his favorite nun might have cast a vote in his selection. He smiled humbly as he explained, "I was no saint, but I tried to be a good kid."

The award in religion, combined with his athletic success, his being voted captain of the varsity track team, and his final grade point average of B+, enabled Patrick to compete for a place in a number of colleges. He gained admission to the state's university, a private college in a neighboring state, and his dream school, a Catholic college in Boston. When news arrived of Patrick's conditional acceptance to the Catholic college, the family was delighted; however, the reality of paying the high tuition and expenses was daunting. Patrick described the moment when the family discussion turned to the astronomical cost of this college. The question "How are you going to do that?" was raised. His older brother Timmy, who had just returned from a tour with the Merchant Marines, "walked into the kitchen and handed me a check for $10,000." Patrick reflected on that poignant moment: "He's 22 years old, and he's giving me $10,000. How do you say thank you for that? Timmy helped me out tremendously."

As Patrick left St. Joseph's, he found it difficult to say goodbye to Rob Casey but remained grateful to his coach. He explained this man's significant influence on his life:

> He was my mentor, my cheerleader, my advocate. He was a port in the storm, a sage, a guy to whom I could turn to for answers. More importantly, he really believed in me. He was someone who genuinely believed that I could succeed. I never thought he was patronizing or pie in the sky. When he talked

> with me he really believed that I could do great things, and I
> started to realize that.

Following a large family celebration for his graduation from St. Joseph's, Patrick continued working at Casey's Roast Beef and enrolled in two summer classes at his new school. He discovered that the college had inaugurated a new initiative admitting a cohort of highly capable students with learning disabilities in a transitional program. Rather than enroll in the traditional 15-hour course load, students would enroll in 12 hours each semester and 6 hours each summer. During his first summer, Patrick completed a sociology course and a writing seminar. Achieving a grade of B in each course resulted in his conditional acceptance to the college becoming an official admission.

Throughout his 4 years as an undergraduate, he benefitted from modifications in curriculum that were provided for his cohort. He explained that students could complete a foreign language requirement through a course in cultural studies. He did not take advantage of other accommodations that were afforded students, such as additional time on exams. He smiled as he explained, "I got the accommodations to get my rear end in the door of [the college], but I didn't have much to do with them in terms of accommodating me throughout my program." He enjoyed his friendships with cohort members: "I was around kids who were using the term 'learning disabled' which was something I was running from. I thought 'These are bright kids, and I was like them.'" He indicated, "The college didn't use that terminology. They described it holistically as a big profile. Whatever the profile was, I fit that profile."

Patrick reflected that his college years were a stressful time. Surrounded by students whose parents paid the astronomical tuition, he was forced to maintain several jobs during his college years. He did not have time for athletics. Instead, he commuted 2 days a week to work at Casey's Roast Beef and returned to work again on weekends. He was also employed as a security guard checking book bags at the college bookstore. He took on a position as a resident assistant in the dormitory in order to benefit from free housing, and he also made extra money videotaping sporting events for the athletic department. He described his experience:

> As I look back on that time, there were years where I made
> $30,000 a year, and I'd be sitting in my dorm room with five

bucks. I had no money, and kids were constantly asking me to go out. I couldn't go. I really didn't enjoy campus life . . . My brothers went to more football games on my student ticket than I did! I was always stressed out about money.

Patrick was proud of how hard he "hustled to get through college." Periodically, his parents were able to provide him some financial support; however he took out significant college loans. He joked, "I have a great friend. Her name is Sallie Mae. She finds me any time I move. I don't even have to tell her I'm moving. She can find me. She must really like me."

Initially, Patrick declared mass communication as his college major and later shifted to special education. Contemplating how he might be of service to others, he asked, "What do I have to offer?" He decided he really wanted to better understand himself and how he learned, as well as help others who faced struggles in school. Hence, his college degree was in education, with a specialization in mild learning disabilities. He enjoyed the theoretical courses in his education program and was fascinated with learning and development; however, his practicum experiences in public school classrooms brought on surprising challenges:

I loved the content. I loved reading about kids and development. There were also some great assessment classes. Reliability and validity. I thought, "This is all good!" But the actual time in the trenches helped me to realize I don't want to do this. I was pretty good relating to kids and getting along with my mentor teacher, but the anxiety and panic attacks would again manifest themselves. Getting up to the board and you don't spell so well. 9 times 8 is . . . diagramming sentences, just struggling with all those issues. To be a [college] student and to get up there and not be able to spell. It was a nightmare. And so I realized, "You know what? I'm no teacher. I'm still quirky. It didn't go away." I didn't understand twice-exceptional at that time. I just knew one side of it, and that was something to be ashamed of and to hide.

During this difficult period in his junior year, Patrick's mother was diagnosed with cancer. Mrs. Brennan's prognosis was that she had 6 months to live. Patrick described his response to the news: "That was very hard, because where would I be without her?" His memories of his senior year were more "foggy and miserable" as he persevered with classes, working at the restaurant, student teaching, and many trips home on weekends to spend time with his dying mother. "Everything was on autopilot, but by that point I had command of myself as a student to step to the line and finish the drill." During this dark period in his life, he met Jenna Dattalo, another resident assistant in the dormitory, and they began dating.

During his final semester, Patrick was scheduled to be observed in a special education classroom. Spending time at home with his mother, he overlooked this commitment in his calendar. As a result of this absence, the instructor was unwilling to reschedule the observation of his teaching; hence, he did not complete the special education teaching credential. Frustrated with this situation and having decided that K–12 teaching was not his forté, he chose not to fight the battle and agreed to forsake the Bachelor of Science degree. Instead he would graduate with a Bachelor of Arts degree in Education with the concentration in learning disabilities. He concluded, "I lost the teaching credential, but I have a degree from [a well respected Catholic] College with a 3.3 GPA. I finished it up."

Life After College

Patrick's mother died in March of his senior year, and during her final days, she made him promise that he would not return home to his father. Concerned that her husband was drinking heavily and not in a good psychological state of mind, she begged Patrick to move on with his life. Following his graduation from college, he visited his older sister in North Carolina. She had started a consulting firm that specialized in providing adventure-based training experiences and workshops for corporate groups and K–12 student groups. She provided him an opportunity to work for the firm delivering workshops that featured ropes courses and team building. Patrick maintained that during the yearlong period of grieving, his sister really "took care" of him. He found that he enjoyed teaching the ropes courses and leading adult corporate groups. He appreciated his sister's support: "I am forever grateful to her. With that opportunity I developed some skills that were later utilized heavily." During that period, Jenna was hired as a special education teacher in a North Carolina community, and within that year, she and Patrick were engaged to be married.

Following their wedding, Jenna's professional goals of pursuing a graduate program led them to return to her university hometown to pursue her master's degree in education. She was employed in the local public schools, and Patrick succeeded in gaining admission to a master's program in adult education. He interviewed well and again was accepted into the program on a conditional basis. He made connections with the outdoor recreation program on campus and secured a graduate assistantship facilitating ropes courses that allowed the newlyweds significant financial savings. He earned his degree in 2 years and achieved a 4.0 grade point average. He indicated that he thoroughly enjoyed the program and found it exhilarating to be in an academic environment again. "I really started to shine. The adult education department could not have been more tailored to my strengths. There were no in-class exams. I'm slow and deliberate, and I can write thoughtful papers. I've got to have time to think."

At this point in his life, Patrick had learned significant strategies for success. He explained that he did "a lot of reconnaissance work" in looking for instructors who he believed would be student-centered. When it was time to pursue the required course in statistics, he enrolled in it during the summer when he could take it in isolation. He partnered with an international graduate student whose strength was statistics. She helped him prepare for exams, and in turn, he supported her with conceptual organization of the theoretical papers she was required to write in her second language.

As he was approaching the conclusion of his program, one of his professors, Marie Howard, encouraged him to apply to the doctoral program in adult education. He explained, "The ropes course stuff was great, but I was really reading so much scholarly literature and enjoying it. I was growing and developing and learning so much. I wanted more." Upon admission to the program, he was offered another graduate assistantship in which he provided university community outreach services. Patrick thrived on providing rural school districts and community groups throughout the state with leadership development workshops on topics that incorporated "experiential, hands-on, group dynamics" training. He pointed out that these were topics he was passionate about. Dr. Howard, who also served as his doctoral mentor, delighted in reporting that Patrick's workshop evaluations were far superior to those of the faculty.

He suffered a blow when Dr. Howard announced that she was retiring from the university. Patrick went in search of a new major professor and found Dr. Susan Morrison. He described his new advisor as "intimidating" and not the "warm, fuzzy nurturer" to whom he typically gravitated. Instead, Dr. Morrison was rigorous and expected excellence from her doctoral protégés. Patrick eventually appreciated her style and was grateful for her efforts in keeping him focused throughout the dissertation process. He described a typical meeting with her:

> She caught on to me in terms of my being scattered. I can sugarcoat excuses and dance around deadlines, but she said, "Cut the crap! Pull your calendar out. On the 14th, write my name down. You're meeting with me. You're bringing me Chapter 2." . . . I wouldn't have graduated without her.

The dedication page in Patrick's dissertation reads, "Thank you, Mom, for your unwavering faith in my ability to achieve." Mrs. Brennan would have been proud of her son, as Patrick's qualitative dissertation research was aligned with his passionate interests. His work examined the transfer of learning from outdoor adventure-based programs to professional environments. Following the university's commencement ceremony, during which Patrick was officially hooded for his Ed.D. degree, the Datallo family gathered for a huge family celebration. Although he had earlier refused to be present for his son's wedding because of an emotional quarrel with Patrick's wife's siblings, Patrick's father surprised the Datallos and arrived for the graduation party. Patrick reflected, "My dad's head was about to cave in, he was just out-of-his-skull proud. He kept saying: 'I can't believe this!'" He continued, "As proud as he was of my older brother at Dartmouth, he was more proud of what I did because of where I came from to where I arrived."

Epilogue

Shortly after earning his doctoral degree, Patrick was employed as a private educational consultant. When asked to describe his work, he explained, "As a consultant, my primary focus was working with and on behalf of students who are bright who have learning problems. I designed some programs geared directly toward the kids. I also worked with adults who shape their world." More recently he has been employed in university public service outreach where his focus is youth leadership development. Today, he designs and delivers programs to support individuals with high-incidence disabilities, particularly attention deficits and learning disabilities, in their efforts to experience academic and life success. In talking about his work with this population of young people, he shared important lessons from his own life:

> When I talk with students, I use a PowerPoint presentation that includes a quote, "It's the double-edged sword of the label." I tell kids that the term *learning disability* is kind of a necessary evil. The label gets you into places and services that you need, but if you're not careful, the double-edged label can cut you, too. You can self-identify as LD. You can dwell on that too much. So I tell them that it's a weapon, and I want you to use the label to tear down barriers. If you've got the LD label or twice-exceptional and it allows you to take a test untimed or some other kind of accommodation, take advantage of those opportunities. If you can listen to your textbooks on an iPod rather than read the book, that's great! It's a double-edged sword, so don't get cut by the label and let it bleed all over you. Use it as a weapon to cut down barriers and get what you need in this world.

CONCLUSION

WHAT HAVE WE LEARNED FROM THESE TALENTED YOUNG MEN?

All the world is full of suffering. It is also full of overcoming.
— Helen Keller

A popular quote that often appears on refrigerator magnets is Vivian Greene's message: "Life isn't about waiting for the storm to pass. It's about learning to dance in the rain." The five talented young men featured in this book endured more than a storm. They faced torrential hurricane rains and wind. The life portraits of Joseph, Keith, Dante, Sebastian, and Patrick are inspirational, for these men certainly "danced in the rain" and faced their challenges with courage. Their crippling situations with adversity throughout childhood and adolescence did not impede the development of their talents. They were not from privileged backgrounds. All five came from working class or low-income families. These men were able to rise above their troubles to make significant contributions to society and enjoy meaningful lives. Their resilience enabled them to overcome problems that would overwhelm most individuals and drive them to despair. In order to understand just how strong these men were, it is critical that we understand the role of resilience in their lives. What follows is a brief discussion of resilience theory to guide our understanding.

Understanding Resilience

Resilience has gained much attention over several decades since scholars observed that individuals could cope and adapt in spite of adversity. The operational definition of resilience has been widely debated. Scholars and theorists disagree as to whether resilience is a personality characteristic, a process that a person undergoes, or an outcome that a person reaches. To highlight the similarities and differences in definitions of resilience, several are provided below:

- Werner (2015) defined it as "the dynamic process that leads to positive adaptation within the context of significant adversity" (p. 4).
- Masten and Reed (2002) explained it as "a class of phenomena characterized by patterns of positive adaptation in the context of significant adversity or risk" (p. 75).
- Neihart (2002) viewed it as an individual's "ability to achieve emotional health and social competence in spite of a history of adversity and stress" (p. 114).
- Ahern, Ark, and Byers (2008) regarded it as "an adaptive, stress-resistant personal quality that permits one to thrive in spite of adversity" (p. 32).
- Neenan (2018) explained it as a combination of flexible cognitive, behavioral, and emotional responses to acute or chronic adversity.

Although definitions have long been debated, there is little dispute that there are individuals whom most people would consider resilient by almost any definition, and findings from diverse fields point to the same conclusions with undeniable consistency (Masten & Reed, 2002).

In thinking about resilience, consider two important questions: What is it in a person's life that places someone at risk for poor outcomes? What in life protects someone from poor outcomes? Comprehensive research studies on resilience have focused on risk and protective factors (Werner, 2015; Williams, Bryan, Morrison, & Scott, 2017; Zimmerman et al., 2013). These factors are circumstances or influences that contribute to the development of human beings in positive or negative ways. Risk factors increase an individual's vulnerability, and protective factors buffer individuals from the harmful impact of difficult circumstances. For example, poverty places young people at risk for poor outcomes (e.g., dropping out of school), while supportive families serve as protection for young people (e.g., completion of college degrees).

Scholars have maintained that resilience is dynamic, as it constantly changes over time. They have also indicated that resilience is developmental, because an individual grows and develops in response to struggles in life, and it may be influenced by one's environment (Ahern et al., 2008).

Neenan (2018), a cognitive therapist, highlighted several significant points to consider. He maintained that an important concept to take into account is that resilience is not a fixed attribute. If an individual is hardened by difficult times, he is not invulnerable. No matter how robust a person becomes by managing life's challenges, that individual still remains vulnerable to coping poorly with adversity in the future. We need to understand that vulnerability does not constitute weakness, for none of us maintain complete resistance to adversity, and perfection is not expected. Moreover, resilience does not remain fixed—when circumstances change, resilience changes.

Psychologists often use examples of individuals who not only overcome adversity, but also move on to scale the heights of personal achievement in their professional domain. Neenan (2018) pointed out that these paragons of resilience are an extraordinary few and highlighted that we need to consider the people who cope with the ups and downs of daily life, taking on difficult problems and facing inevitable adversities. He also called attention to the difference between the survivor and the resilient individual. He maintained that a survivor can become consumed with bitterness, while a resilient person displays personal growth and pursues important goals. According to Neenan, the term *resilient* emphasizes that people do more than merely get through difficult emotional experiences; they become involved in the process of self-righting and growth. He posited that all humans have the capacity to become resilient and noted that resilience skills could be taught and nurtured (see also Newman, 2003; Papházy, 2003).

Neenan (2018) also highlighted that when individuals face a time of crisis, those who pride themselves on sturdy self-reliance may view seeking help from others as a sign of weakness when it is not. A misconception of resilience is the idea that it is found exclusively within a person. Resilience is not developed in social isolation. When support is offered, individuals should take the opportunity to benefit from it, as help from others may reduce the duration of a struggle to overcome a challenge.

Some may think of resilient people as stoic individuals who refuse to show emotion in the face of pain and suffering or reach out to others for support. Resilience is actually about managing emotions and not suppressing them (Neenan, 2018). Adverse events in one's life are apt to trigger negative emotions, and these feelings will need to be worked through in order to find adaptive responses to the negative events. Resilience depends on being flexible when one responds to adverse events. We cannot remain stuck in negative feelings and allow them to paralyze us. These emotions serve as important sources of information that something is seriously wrong in one's life and need attention.

Discovering positive meaning from one's challenges in life is an important issue in resilience. Psychologists suggest that people who have gone through dark times derive benefit from them in three ways (Haidt, 2006). These benefits are collectively referred to as *post-traumatic growth* (Boniwell, 2006). The first benefit is a positive change in one's self-image. Rising to meet the challenge of adversity may draw upon unexpected abilities, which may change the way an individual sees oneself. A second benefit involves relationships that become clarified and enriched. When times are tough, we begin to see who are fair-weather friends and who are all-weather friends. During tough times, presumed good friends may disappear, and invaluable supportive relationships may surprise us. The third benefit is an alteration of our priorities. A new perspective following trauma often emerges and forces one to take inventory regarding what is most important in life (Neenan, 2018).

Adversity in the Lives of Joseph, Keith, Sebastian, Dante, and Patrick

It is difficult to be a young male in this country. This message has long been reported in the popular press, and scholars claim that the destructive effects of society's failure to recognize boys' emotional needs are becoming evident in school and beyond (Howes, 2017; O'Neil, 2015). This problem becomes more complex for gifted males (Hébert,

2012b, 2013). Add to that complexity the adverse circumstances faced by the talented young men in this study. Having met Joseph, Keith, Sebastian, Dante, and Patrick, we can agree that surviving adolescence without parents, and experiencing poverty, alcoholic family members, ongoing psychological and physical abuse, bullying and gay bashing, racism, and negotiating school with learning disabilities were seriously adverse conditions that remained with the men for long periods of time and added complexity to their lives. As we reflect on the adversity faced by these men, we should attempt to place ourselves in their individual situations and think about how we might have responded to such circumstances.

Joseph described many poignant moments in his experience. He sobbed as he left his extended family in the South to move to New England with his father. For years, he lived life as a latchkey child. It had to be very difficult to learn of his mother's past with drug dealing. The experience of watching his father attempt to fix a problem with serious consequences was certainly traumatic for Joseph. We can only imagine how he must have felt as he watched his father being escorted out of the courtroom in handcuffs and later visited his father in jail. It had to be devastating for Joseph to receive the final phone call from his father at the airport on the day his father was sent home to Nigeria. The courage Joseph displayed as he then went on to negotiate his life as a high school and university student without any immediate family members available to support him was impressive. Joseph's response to his father's incarceration was consistent with what researchers have noted in adolescent experiences with parents being in prison. Scholars have found that young people faced with this situation often implement a strategy of strength and control as a coping mechanism (Johnson & Easterling, 2015). During such a difficult period, teenagers find strength by maintaining some control over their lives. They realize that although they cannot control their parents' incarceration, they can control their own lives. Joseph's strategy was to remain focused on his academic life and his intense schedule of high school extracurricular activities. His dedication to what was happening at school may have enabled him to compartmentalize the various aspects of his complex adolescent life and prevented him from being overwhelmed by his father's situation.

Keith's challenges involved being born into a culture of poverty. His graphic description of the 6-month period when he and his family ate nothing but beans and cornbread was distressing. His family's economic vulnerability resulted in so many transitions throughout his childhood and adolescence, and Keith often felt as though he did not fit into the cultural context of his neighborhood or school. He captured his difficult circumstances as he explained, "I was not a rich White kid, and I wasn't a student of color, which meant I fit in with nobody." His descriptions of the serious bullying he faced at school were poignant. Throughout his adolescence, he seemed lost when he was forced to confront his family's dysfunction as his parents struggled to control his rebellious sister. He believed his parents were unable to understand his developmental needs in adolescence, as they were overwhelmed with their difficult financial circumstances. Keith's experience was aligned with what scholars have noted regarding economically vulnerable families who are forced to move in and out of high-poverty neighborhoods. They maintain that experiencing multiple moves during early or middle childhood is stressful and results in negative outcomes in school (Roy, McCoy, & Raver, 2014). Keith's experience with his family also parallels what Peterson (1997) found in a group of high-ability students from difficult home environments. She noted that they although they had confused and ambivalent feelings about their parents, they remained loyal and enmeshed in the family's distressful situation.

Sebastian's story was heart-wrenching. As the child of an alcoholic parent, he was forced to survive and protect his siblings in an impoverished household filled with tension. We cannot fathom how difficult it would be to deal with the physical and emotional abuse that his father directed toward his disabled mother. We can only respond emotionally when Sebastian described the violence in his home, stating, "That part of my life was so dark, and I felt like I was at such a loss. I didn't want to be there. I didn't see the point of being alive. I just wanted to die." The despair expressed by Sebastian highlights the negative outcomes that researchers have found occur when parental drinking problems directly affect children. Children of alcoholics often struggle with depression, anxiety, suicidal ideation, substance abuse, or challenges with interpersonal relationships (Park & Schepp 2015). Although Sebastian's personal strength was remarkable, his desperation came to a peak when he pleaded with his mother to leave his father and threatened to call the Department of Social Services to have him and his sisters removed from his home. Throughout those horrific years at

Conclusion

home, Sebastian also faced difficult experiences at school. Being one of five African American students among 190 students in his class, he encountered racism as he received verbal attacks from "the redneck racist Southern White boys" in his community. His calm demeanor as he shared those painful experiences with me was stunning and provided evidence of internal strength. Sebastian's experience with racism is consistent with what many African American adolescent males undergo in schools (Bridges, 2013, Maddox, 2013) and highlights the challenges that educators face in creating schools where all students feel welcome and diversity is celebrated.

Dante was courageous. He sat in his living room with his head wrapped in bandages and shared his life-threatening experience with his craniotomy. He did so with quiet calmness, and I knew immediately that I was having a conversation with a very special individual. To have survived such a terrifying health challenge and be able to discuss his experience with such composure was astounding. The adversity Dante experienced as a young child who lost both parents and moved to another part of the country where so few children looked like him was difficult. Discovering that he needed hearing aids early on could not have been easy. The challenges he and his siblings faced in transitioning to his aunt's household were most difficult. The struggle he faced in dealing with his homosexuality in an intolerable home and the gay bashing he experienced at school throughout his elementary, middle, and high school years were painful. Dante's experiences were parallel to what researchers have reported regarding gay adolescent males facing ridicule, verbal abuse, sexual taunting, and mock rape in schools (Beckerman, 2017; Friedrichs, 2018; Lipkin, 2001), and the unwillingness of educators to intervene and come to the support of gay students (Shelton & Barnes, 2016). Dante's search to find a place where he fit in within his school was a constant challenge. Finally, the psychological and physical abuse he experienced at the hands of his aunt and her partner reached a point where he had to escape from the community. His vivid description of the night he escaped from home and how he managed to survive as a runaway indicated how critical an event that evening was in his life. Dante's story was both complex and inspiring. His experiences mirror those described by researchers who found that teenage runaways leave to gain control of their lives by changing their situations with emotionally abusive homes. They develop new friendships to find safety and sustenance and often learn from their experience that they are unable to run from their problems (Flowers, 2010; Martinez, 2006).

Patrick's story was filled with anxiety, emotional tension, depression, and what he called "chronic success deprivation." The poignant scenarios Patrick shared were far more serious than a typical teenager's experience with adolescent angst. He certainly faced a challenge as a twice-exceptional student to form an identity as a bright young man with learning disabilities. For Patrick, growing up as the youngest boy in a large family of highly competitive siblings with several older brothers who were viewed as high-powered role models was difficult. As an adolescent, he certainly compared himself to his siblings and believed he did not measure up to his family's standards. The anxiety he experienced in school every day as he struggled to comprehend why he was having such a hard time understanding what was happening in the classroom became overwhelming. His descriptions of the heart palpitations, the sweating, and the panic attacks he experienced were graphic. His alcoholic father's response to his lack of success in school was also unnerving and caused more stress. The transitions he was forced to make from public to parochial school and dropping back a grade level would be devastating to any middle school student, but Patrick had no other options. His explanation of how he negotiated his high school and university years was impressive; however, even though he enjoyed success in athletics and thrived socially, his academic journey remained bumpy throughout his schooling. Patrick's experience with "chronic success deprivation," and his anxiety, emotional tension, and depression were comparable to what Baum, Schader, and Owen (2017) found in their work with twice-exceptional students. They called attention to a growing population of students who, although intellectually capable, talented, or creative, are simultaneously burdened with learning differences that make traditional schooling a miserable experience. These students' advanced abilities combined with challenging disabilities result in a paradoxical situation for them, and educators and parents must understand what can occur when working with combinations of exceptionalities—both strengths and complex challenges.

What Influenced and Sustained the Resilience?

The two questions I asked throughout this research were what enabled these talented young men to overcome the adversity, and what were the factors that influenced the emergence and sustainability of their resilience? Several significant themes across the life stories of the five men emerged in my analysis and help to answer these questions (as discussed in the sections that follow):

- Teachers who recognized promise and invested significant efforts
- Developing talents through extracurricular activities and athletics
- Interwoven personal characteristics
- At home in college: Finding community and shaping identity

Teachers who recognized promise and invested significant efforts. The five young men in this study benefitted from the emotional support of caring adults in their lives. These individuals emerged from different areas of the young mens' adolescent experiences. They were varied: school paraprofessionals, coaches in afterschool sports, advisers from extracurricular activities, guidance counselors, and social workers. In addition, the five men benefitted from K–12 teachers who took a serious interest in their emotional well-being. Although the men all referred to teachers who challenged them intellectually and held high expectations for them academically, they especially appreciated what these teachers did to support emotional well-being when the men were faced with difficult challenges in their personal lives. These teachers listened, provided encouragement and guidance, and intervened with bureaucratic systems for their students when they faced difficult challenges. These teachers did more than address emotional well-being; they encouraged the development of talents in the young men, whether it was directing them to extracurricular activities and programs that would nurture their strengths or serving as personal cheerleaders for them as they competed in academic and athletic domains.

Within the collection of supportive adults and teachers, there emerged one particular teacher who was especially critical to the success of each of the men in this study. Each young man was fortunate to have one teacher who recognized his promise and invested significant personal energy and time in supporting him. Essentially, these teachers went above and beyond what most K–12 educators would do for students and made certain that these talented males would move beyond their difficult challenges to reach a better place in life. Some might argue that these educators were "lifesavers" in that what they did for these young men had such a positive impact on them—their life trajectories were shifted in a positive direction because of these teachers.

Joseph appreciated a number of caring adults early in his childhood. He benefitted from the intervention of Mrs. Wilson, his fourth- and fifth-grade teacher who took extra time to inquire about what was going on in his life, provided him rides to school, and even invited him to join her family's summer vacation trip. He was also grateful for Mr. Gagliano in middle school, who got him involved in the school's drama productions, and Mr. Hannigan, a high school teacher who advocated for him when administrators were discussing possibly transferring him to an alternative high school. Another high school teacher, Mr. Marshall, quietly wrote a check to cover the cost of Joseph's band field trip to Disney World. Joseph was fortunate to have another important adult who became a personal mentor. Solomon Okafor, the National Society for Black Engineers university chapter liaison to Joseph's high school, was a role model who provided him guidance during the college search, application, and admission process.

The one teacher who went the extra mile for Joseph was Sara Coleman, his high school math teacher, who spotted his leadership talents and encouraged him to use them in a proactive manner. Sara served as a counselor to Joseph during his difficult times. She invested much of her personal energy when she connected Joseph to her family. Sara, her husband, and her father played an important role in providing Joseph emotional support by inviting him to join their family's home renovation project on weekends, a time when they could talk with him about his father's deportation lawsuit. As Joseph compartmentalized his life during his father's challenging legal battles, the only time he was able to talk openly about his father's difficult situation was when he was engaged in the home construction work. Sara and her family remained Joseph's loyal supporters long after his father was deported.

Keith had several important teachers who looked out for his emotional well-being early on. He reflected on a warm and supportive second-grade teacher. In fifth grade, he was inspired by Dr. Dow, who quietly let him know how he valued his mathematical abilities, and in sixth grade was appreciative of Mr. Eastman, who handed him a copy of *The Island on Bird Street,* an important book that helped Keith gain some self-understanding. Mr. Warner, his high school drama teacher, was the teacher who helped him "find his voice" and remained a strong supporter all through school.

The teacher who was most personally invested in Keith's development was Mr. Beale, the debate coach who inspired him, trained him in debate, provided emotional support, and remained a mentor long after high school. Mr. Beale was also responsible for connecting Keith to Dan Truman, the university debate coach who was able to recruit Keith to his program with a university fellowship and also served as a personal and professional mentor to him. Keith remained in touch with Mr. Beale long after his college graduation and maintained that he would not have achieved his success as a college debate coach without Mr. Beale's significant investment in his talents.

Sebastian was blessed to have caring adults beyond his immediate family who influenced him. His loving grandmother played an important role. She attempted to protect him from his dysfunctional home situation and supported his emotional well-being while encouraging him to escape his family's impoverished situation by acquiring a good education.

Sebastian also benefitted from a number of emotionally supportive teachers during his K–12 years. He appreciated several of his middle school teachers who recognized his talents and a number of high school educators who were supportive. He responded to the teaching style of his precalculus teacher, and he developed important relationships with the teachers who wrote letters of recommendation for his admission to the university math and science academy. He celebrated those relationships when he invited those teachers to a luncheon before his departure for the academy. He was grateful to his physics teacher, who called his attention to the call for applicants to the newly established math and science academy, and he appreciated all Ms. Bowden, his guidance counselor, did for him throughout his high school years. Sebastian also highlighted the important influence the academy's director had on him through his counseling and inspirational seminars.

The educator who invested significantly in Sebastian's development was Ms. Gaston, his Upward Bound teacher, who worked with him throughout high school and made certain that he was involved in the Upward Bound summer program at the university for several summers.

Ms. Gaston recognized Sebastian's potential and was determined to help him overcome his difficult circumstances at home. To support him, she personally drove Sebastian and his mother to the university campus for his admissions interview to the math and science academy. His senior year spent at the academy essentially shifted his life's trajectory to success.

Dante also reflected on emotionally supportive teachers. Mrs. Callahan, his third-grade teacher who recognized his creative strengths, was important to him. The paraprofessional in her classroom who recognized his artistic abilities was also important to him when she provided him with a sketchbook and crayons to nurture what she saw as a special gift in art. Mrs. Branford, the enrichment specialist, also supported his creative talents and strong musical ability. He was grateful for his high school guidance counselor's support when he ran away from home and she was able to facilitate the negotiation of his return to his community through the Department of Child and Protective Family Services (CPFS). During his university experience, he valued the training and emotional support of the highly respected musicians who mentored him, Dr. Agostini and Dr. Mancini. Dante also recognized that several other adults played important roles in his overcoming his circumstances. He would not have succeeded without the help and support of Elizabeth, his foster mother, and her husband; his stepsister Cindy, who assisted him with his escape from home and connected him to support systems in the gay community; his case manager in the CPFS system; and his partner, Robert, who was critical to his success in graduate school.

Dante's relationship with his music teacher was reserved; however, it was Mr. Kendall who invested significantly in the talented young man who wanted to play the bassoon. When he learned of Dante's interest in learning this instrument, he went in search of one within the school district. When he succeeded in acquiring one, he began individual instruction with Dante. In providing Dante the opportunity to experiment with the bassoon, Mr. Kendall worked closely with him in perfecting his performance. He arranged for Dante to compete at the highest levels statewide and in regional competitions. In addition to the individual bassoon lessons, Dante enjoyed a daily music class with Mr. Kendall and went on to place as first chair clarinet, first chair bass clarinet, and oboe. Finally, Mr. Kendall personally introduced Dante to his professional mentor at the university, Dr. Agostini, the internationally acclaimed bassoonist. Mr. Kendall was proud to send his star student to study with his mentor. When Dante made the decision to pursue early college entrance, Dr. Agostini was delighted to receive him as a new protégé. Mr. Kendall's significant intervention into Dante's schooling occurred at a critical time, the middle and high school years when the bullying and gay bashing he experienced was severe.

Patrick recognized two nuns in his parochial school experience who supported him emotionally: Sister Alice, the principal of his middle school, who appreciated his struggles as a student and provided him the opportunity to be the school's photographer, and Sister Anne, the director of the campus ministry office in his high school, who spent time counseling him. He also found support from the pediatric researcher at Children's Hospital Boston who delivered an important message—to always think of himself as a very smart boy. Along with his loving wife Jenna, he received strong support from Dr. Howard and Dr. Morrison, two professors in his graduate school years who were influential in reaching his goal of obtaining his doctoral degree.

Rob Casey was the educator who invested a tremendous amount of energy to support Patrick. Receiving the "The Full Casey Treatment" had a powerful influence on Patrick's emotional well-being. This gentleman, who arranged to have Patrick assigned to a different guidance counselor, served as his social studies teacher, track coach, unofficial mentor, and eventually provided him a part-time job in his family-owned seafood restaurant, certainly influenced Patrick's trajectory for success after high school. The relationship with Rob Casey was one that shaped Patrick as a young man and continues to influence him as a professional. His experience with Coach Casey is parallel to Hébert's (1995) findings in an ethnographic study of Coach Brogan, an urban high school swim coach who had a significant influence on the academic achievement of high-ability males. Brogan was known as a caring adult who incorporated a counseling component into his athletic program and nurtured individual excellence. Athletes described him as a father figure or mentor who developed supportive relationships with them and focused on their academic, athletic, and personal development as gifted young men. Rob Casey's intervention with Patrick and Coach Brogan's philosophical approach to coaching young men were consistent with a finding in a more recent study of award-winning football coaches. Researchers in sports psychology found that award-winning high school football

133

coaches saw the coaching of life skills as inseparable from coaching strategies for the enhancement of athletic skills. For these coaches, the personal development of their players was top priority (Gould, Collins, Lauer, & Chung, 2007).

Developing talents through extracurricular activities and athletics. Another important theme across the five life stories of the young men was their involvement in extracurricular activities and talent development opportunities beyond the classroom. It is important to understand that involvement in extracurricular activities that produce tangible products or performances—such as precision marching in color guard groups, musical concerts and competitions, debate competitions, high school track championships, or the organization and facilitation of a new high school club—builds a sense of accomplishment and success. Prosocial activities provide young men with evidence that something can be gained by persevering. Such experiences also demonstrate that choices matter, effort does make a difference, and adults value what young people do with their talents (Heath & McLaughlin, 1993; Reis, Colbert, & Hébert, 2005). When students become involved in meaningful extracurricular activities, they develop relationships with adults who influence how they see themselves. These important extracurricular groups provide students with an adult who sees them as young adults, cares for them as individuals, and serves as a mentor, critic, or advocate (Hébert, 2011).

From the scholarship on identity development in gifted students, we understand that extracurricular activities play an important role in shaping identity (Bucknavage & Worrell, 2005; Olszewski-Kubilius & Lee, 2004). Involvement in clubs, musical groups, teams, or campaigns provides opportunities for intelligent young people to build a sense of self-efficacy and success (Calvert & Cleveland, 2006; Hébert & Reis, 1999). A strong sense of self evolves from being a member of a group noted for accomplishment. These group experiences enable teenagers to construct a positive view of self and raise their aspirations for the future (Hébert, 2011). Another resilience-building benefit is the opportunity to find others with similar interests—through their extracurricular activities, young people are able to build important friendships with others who appreciate their passions. For twice-exceptional students like Patrick, extracurricular activities provide salvation. Rather than seeing themselves as intelligent young people who may be struggling learners in math or language arts, they prefer to see themselves as superstars on the athletic field or the theatrical stage. Their engagement in a sport or extracurricular activity provides them the feeling of what it must be like to be a smart student. Their identity is shaped by their experiences with such successes.

Joseph engaged in drama, athletics, and student leadership. Keith became an actor and debater. Sebastian performed in the color guard. Dante competed in a variety of creative and academic competitions and excelled in music. Patrick outshined his competitors in cross-country and track. Extracurricular activities, summer programs, and involvement in athletics were all important outlets for discovering strengths and developing talents. The men described how these activities were also outlets for managing the stressors in their lives. When faced with difficult challenges at home or in their personal lives, they could take their minds off of their situations, focus their energy on something positive, and direct their energy in meaningful productivity. Several of the men recognized that their involvement in activities enabled them to ward off depression, and they described how their involvement allowed them to compartmentalize their lives in a way that helped them to "block out" their problems and thrive in activities that nurtured their talents.

The talent development opportunities provided the men with experiences with success. Such success provided them with the positive emotional feelings that allowed them to fill the "emotional gas tanks" that fueled their resilience. Their involvement in extracurricular activities also helped to expose them to a world beyond their local contexts. The exposure to college campuses through debate team competition, Upward Bound summer camp, and music and athletic competitions enabled them to get a quick peek into what life might look once they left their difficult situations at home.

Interwoven personal characteristics. Researchers who explore resilience maintain that protective factors include internal qualities or characteristics in individuals (Masten & Reed, 2002). This phenomenon emerged as a theme in this study. The five men benefitted from a number of interwoven personal characteristics that supported them in developing resilience. These personal characteristics were linked and played a role in supporting the men in coping with their adversity. Each of the young men maintained strong perseverance. They displayed a sense of future-mindedness. Practical intelligence also contributed to their survival

135

and success. They benefitted from their intensity, and having a sense of empathy was also evident in their experiences.

Perseverance. Perseverance is a characteristic of talented individuals—a steadfastness in doing something in spite of difficulty or delay in achieving success. This attribute was evident in all five of the young men. Joseph's perseverance was evident in his dedication to his academic and extracurricular life in high school, his devotion to working on behalf of his father in pursuing the materials he needed to pursue the immigration case, and his dedication to his church group both in high school and while at the university. Joseph's final pursuit of an advanced graduate degree is another fine example of his tenacity.

Determination and perseverance were evident in Keith's involvement in debate as a high school student and throughout his college years and early career. Sebastian's perseverance was obvious early in his elementary school years. His dedication to his studies and his conscientious approach to school supported him as he was forced to negotiate the ugly challenges he faced at home. Sebastian's intensity in all aspects of his life highlights his determination, whether it was excelling academically as a young elementary student, thriving in math acceleration, or competing fiercely in his role as a member of the color guard in his university's marching band.

Dante's story was one of courage and perseverance. We see this in his experiences as a child in elementary school striving to be the best in everything he did. In middle and high school this appeared in his pursuit of excellence in his science fair competition, speech contest, invention convention, and Odyssey of the Mind competition, and his determination to contribute his hard work and dedication in track. Throughout his middle, high school, and university experience, he dedicated endless hours in pursuing perfection as a classical musician. Dante's pursuit of advanced graduate degrees in two different professional fields was testimony to his tenacity and determination.

Patrick's spunk and perseverance are unmistakable in overcoming what he referred to as his "chronic success deprivation" through his athletic involvement in both football and track. With the support he received from his coach and his new philosophy of "step to the line," Patrick made a pledge to himself and took on tough challenges with determined effort, enabling him to eventually earn honor roll status in his junior year of high school. This fortitude was also evident in his pursuit of his undergraduate and graduate degrees.

Several of the men displayed what Angela Duckworth and her colleagues (Duckworth, Peterson, Matthews, & Kelly, 2007), have labeled *grit*—"the perseverance and passion for long term goals" (p. 1087). Duckworth (2016) explained that "Grit is about working on something you care about so much that you're willing to stay loyal to it . . . it's doing what you love, but not just falling in love—staying in love" (p. 56). Her research studies have determined that grit has two components—passion and perseverance—and when applied to a long-term objective, individuals accomplish great things. Reflecting on the experiences of the men in this study, one might argue that they were in the developmental process of building the perseverance that today would be labeled grit. To highlight one example, consider Dante's pursuit of his professional goals in music. He fell in love with the bassoon, dedicated himself to endless hours of practice, stayed in love with the music, and eventually succeeded in meeting his goal of performing in well-known venues in Manhattan. Duckworth (2016) maintained that grit can become strengthened. She explained,

> grit grows as we figure out our life philosophy, learn to dust ourselves off after rejection and disappointment, and learn to tell the difference between low-level goals that should be abandoned quickly and higher-level goals that demand more tenacity. The maturation story is that we develop the capacity for long-term passion and perseverance as we get older" (p. 82).

We see maturation in Dante's dedication to his music and again in his shift to the nursing profession, where his perseverance served him well in reaching his goals in a new career. Moreover, we see the developmental maturation of perseverance in the other four men in their pursuit of college degrees and professional careers.

An internal locus of control supported the perseverance evident in the men. Locus of control explains the degree to which an individual perceives a relationship between his own behavior and the outcome of that behavior (Rotter, 1990). A person who assumes control or responsibility for the events in his life is said to display an internal locus of control. Regardless of the serious adversity they encountered, these young men did not blame their less-than-stellar performance on their difficult circumstances. They took control of their personal situations as they moved forward to create better lives for themselves. The internal strength evident in the men in this study matches what Hébert (2000) found in a group of younger high-achieving urban high school males who faced adversity in adolescence, and a population of high-achieving African American males in a predominantly White university (Hébert, 2002) who looked beyond racist experiences in their setting, remained focused on reaching their goals, and went on to create lives of fulfillment.

Future-mindedness. Future-mindedness describes an orientation toward the pursuit and achievement of one's future goals in life (Gallagher, 2009). Scholars in positive psychology maintain that those looking to the future are generally hopeful and hold positive expectations for what lies ahead in life. These individuals work hard in planning for their futures. This characteristic of future-mindedness was evident in the stories of the young men in the study.

Several were provided glimpses into what life might be like for them once they moved away from home and their difficult circumstances. Keith was exposed to the world of higher education when he and his debate teammates competed at an Ivy League institution. Experiencing the elite setting and the students gathered around the free speech area for an anti-war protest seemed to serve as a catalyst for Keith, as it enabled him to craft an image of what a university undergraduate experience would look like. With the new insight he gained from that visit to the university, he became more committed than ever to dedicating his energy to debate competitions, increasing the likelihood of his admission to college. His vision of his future changed, and he began to apply more serious effort to his studies. Future-mindedness was also evident in Sebastian's story as he was exposed to university life as a middle school student enrolled in the Upward Bound program in his school. With several weeks spent on a college campus in the summer months, Sebastian envisioned a college education as his plan for the future. Joseph's experience with a school trip to Disney World enabled him to see a world beyond his difficult urban environment. When he experienced this travel, he was inspired to think more seriously about life after high school. Dante's future-mindedness appeared to be self-initiated. As a result of viewing a particular popular television program, he became intrigued with life in San Francisco and saw his future taking him there. When he became exposed to classical music and discovered the world of internationally renowned conductors, he crafted another dream of studying music and performing in New York City.

Practical intelligence. Practical intelligence was another characteristic evident in the five life stories. Sternberg and his colleagues (2000) explained practical intelligence as the ability that individuals use to find the best fit between themselves and the demands of their environment. We understand this as common sense or capabilities that people need to negotiate their way through life. This characteristic served the men well. For example, Joseph's understanding of the need to compartmentalize his life was an example of this intelligence in action. Compartmentalization is beneficial when used to set aside problems that appear overwhelming so they do not penetrate into other areas of an individual's life. Joseph realized that while in high school he needed to emotionally set aside his thoughts regarding his father's difficult deportation situation and focus his thinking on what he needed to do in school and in his extracurricular activities. Keith applied his practical intelligence as a young child when he established a smart strategy of parking his bicycle close to his elementary school building, knowing that the bullies who terrorized him would be chasing him after school. By having the bike close to his classroom entrance, he was able to escape the bullying. Patrick's practical intelligence was evident in several ways. To protect his image in middle school, he made a point to linger on his way to classes so that his friends did not see him entering the special education classroom that had once been the custodial closet. He also realized early on that "being nice" served him well in managing to survive life in middle school. He understood that a visit with each of his teachers at the end of the day in order to ask questions about his classwork and check on how he was doing in class enabled his teachers to view him as a conscientious student who wanted to do well academically. Patrick's practical intelligence also came in handy as a doctoral student who knew how to respond to his major advisor's tough love approach to his dissertation. Dante's practical intelligence was evident in a number of ways. As a high school student, he knew to acquire his birth certificate and social security card in planning his escape from his troubled household. Later he carried court documents with him that enabled him to sign legal paperwork as a minor, allowing him to move into the university dormitory without a parent or guardian's signature. His practical intelligence was also evident in his shift to nursing as a professional career following his experience as a classical musician.

Intensity. The five men lived with intensity. It was readily apparent that they benefited from an augmented capacity for being active, involved, and energetic (Piechowski, 2013). The intensity was apparent in their enthusiasm, animated conversation, and their high energy and enjoyment of kinesthetic activity. With this boundless energy, they gained great pleasure from endless activity. Others around them often found them overwhelming. We saw this in the descriptions of Sebastian's practice and private rehearsals of his color guard routines and the intensity of his lengthy college study sessions taking him into late evening and early morning. Joseph described the focused energy he dedicated to many extracurricular activities in high school. Keith found his voice in drama and then channeled his intensity in debate in high school, college, and his early career. Dante maintained lengthy daily practice sessions as a bassoonist in his music degree programs. His high energy was focused on his music studies; however, earlier in his schooling, his intensity was apparent in many creative and academic competitions. Patrick's intensity was unmistakable in his dedication to athletics. When his coach inspired Patrick to take on his "step to the line" philosophy, the intensity increased.

Talented individuals living with intensity often maintain high expectations for themselves (Hébert, 2011), and this was certainly true of the five men. We saw Joseph's striving to be a leader in so many aspects of his high school year career, and Sebastian's conscientious approach to his studies and precise and perfectionistic approach to his color guard performances. We recognized this trait in Keith's competitiveness and determination to excel in debate. We noted this in Dante's approach to winning academic competitions and earning awards and trophies in elementary and middle school, and later his striving to be positioned as first chair in performance orchestras. We also saw this characteristic in Patrick's motivation to maintain his champion status in running track. Where some might argue that the intense demands or expectations the men imposed on themselves bordered on perfectionism, others would maintain that what we saw within the five men was a healthy striving for excellence (Greenspon, 2012; Schuler, 2000).

Empathy. It was apparent that Joseph, Keith, Sebastian, Dante, and Patrick had become empathic males as a result of their difficult life experiences. Empathy is an emotional response that is other-oriented and congruent with the perceived welfare of another person (Batson, Ahmad, Lishner, & Tsang, 2002, p. 485). If someone is thought to be in need, then empathic emotions that emerge include sympathy, compassion, softheartedness, and tenderness (Cassell, 2002). These men saw others in need, and their empathic emotions enabled them to identify with those individuals and evoked an altruistic motivation to help them.

Their empathy was evident in their response to being involved in this research. All five noted how they saw sharing their experiences as a way to serve other young males who may also be faced with difficult challenges in their lives. Keith said, "If there are young men out there who identify with my story, they can know that no matter how dark and depressed they might feel, they have to know that there is light at the end of the tunnel." Patrick referred to his work advocating for twice-exceptional males, and he provided an empathic message to them regarding having a learning disability: "It's a double-edged sword, so don't get cut by the label and have it bleed all over you. Use it as a weapon to cut down the barriers and get what you need in this world." Dante spoke of his desire to advocate for the underdog. He discussed being drawn to the weakest members of society, those who were most shunned. He said, "I have a great deal of empathy for them. I believe that my empathy comes from being a survivor of racism, being a survivor of gay bashing, being a child of child abuse."

Having experienced such strong adversity themselves, they felt empathy for others. Joseph became dedicated to working with his church youth group in mentoring younger children in his community. He also saw a problem his high school peers were facing and felt compelled to address the issue. He saw their frustration with how little the school's guidance department was doing to prepare students for the college search and admission process. Joseph responded by reaching out to the university chapter of the National Society for Black Engineers and worked with its university liaison to create a "College 101" experience in which high school students shadowed a university engineering student for a day. In his reflections on his personal adversity, Joseph explained, "You have to use it to help others. It's not just about you all the time. You have to be able to incorporate your struggles to help other people." Dante worked to support the emotional well-being of LGBT students on his college campus. Patrick dedicated his career to working to help children with learning disabilities. Dante did the same with his professional shift to nursing in order to address the needs of patients afflicted with mental and emotional conflicts and developmental challenges.

At home in college: Finding community and shaping identity. According to O'Neil (2015), "the transition to college is considered one of the most difficult in a young man's life, with personal, social, familial, academic, and emotional issues interacting with leaving home for the first time" (p. 316). The freshman year for many is the ideal time for young men to reflect on their new status as independent adults in a new context. This was especially true for the five men in the study. The home situations they left behind to attend college were not pleasant. All of them dealt with family issues that were challenging; some more so than others. These challenges included the deportation of a parent, poverty, fathers struggling with alcohol problems, dysfunctional siblings, and physical and psychological abuse. All five of the men had reason to feel good about putting their family's problems behind them and beginning a new chapter of their lives at the university level. Within their new homes on college campuses, they could enjoy their new independence and continue their work in developing their talents. As they pursued their studies, they continued developing specific talents by delving into their chosen majors and enjoying involvement in extracurricular activities on campus. In the social context of a university, intellectual achievements and extracurricular activities are highly valued (Hébert, 2011); therefore, the collegiate environments enjoyed by the young men were influential in shaping their identity formation. Whether their outlets for talent development involved high-powered academic courses, athletic teams, musical groups, or leadership and social action projects, the young men were able to see themselves as capable men who could thrive intellectually, athletically, and socially.

Although Patrick could not become involved in extracurricular activities in his undergraduate years because he had to work several jobs to pay for school expenses, he was able to do so later. His discovery of community took place when he enjoyed his cohort of graduate school colleagues in his master's and doctoral degree programs. The other men all flourished in developing their talents during their early collegiate years. Joseph's strong interpersonal skills and talents in leadership became critical to him when he made connections to other university students involved in building the campus church group. With that same group of students, he branched out into the community and dedicated many hours to mentoring programs with children living in difficult environments. Keith described how he found "his tribe" in the debate community in high school and how this group remained his focus all through his undergraduate and graduate programs. He also enjoyed involvement in a Greek fraternity. Sebastian found great enjoyment being involved in the university marching band's color guard. There he was able to pursue his passion for precision performances on the field. He also found a group of like-minded students in the Honors College who supported each other in their pursuit of academic excellence. Dante's discovery of community occurred easily when he arrived on campus and went in search of the gay community of students. His extracurricular experience incorporated numerous activities with the campus LGBT organization. He found support there, as well as from the music school students who were also dedicated to developing their talents in performance.

Through these experiences, the five men discovered communities of like-minded individuals who became important. Friendships emerged naturally. Being connected to others who were passionate about the same interests enabled them to remain engaged in the activities, tapped into their strengths, and further developed their talents, a finding consistent with Hébert's (2006) study of high-achieving gifted males involved in a Greek fraternity and his research on high-achieving first-generation college students from low-income backgrounds (Hébert, 2018a). Acceptance by new friends involved in the various groups certainly helped provide the men with a sense of belonging, control, self-esteem, and psychological well-being—all predictors of resilience in young people (Fiske, 2009; Scarf et al., 2016; Sheldon & Bettencourt, 2002).

Implications

There are important implications from the findings of this study. Let us reflect on what we have learned from the experiences of these talented young men. Understanding and appreciating their experiences should help teachers, counselors, psychologists, as well as K–12 and university administrators, in supporting young people who face serious adversity in their lives. The discussion below highlights the implications of the study's four overarching themes and other significant issues to consider.

Teachers Who Recognized Promise and Invested Significant Efforts

Sara Coleman, Mr. Beale, Ms. Gaston, Mr. Kendall, and Coach Casey were the teachers we would label "livesavers." These five individuals played a significant role in the shaping a life. They may not have realized just how powerful their influence was on the young men. Their humanitarian approach to their profession is what we would like to see in all educators. These teachers really went the extra mile and made a significant difference. When we consider the complex challenges that educators encounter in their classrooms today, there can be no doubt that these five teachers were very special. Questions that we might ask are: How did they come to be this way? What in their lives influenced them to become so nurturing? How did their personal philosophies shape their work with young people? Answers to these questions would help us create better school experiences for all young people. Another research study to conduct!

The stories of these five teachers and others like them need to be shared with other K–12 educators, school counselors, and school administrators; college of education faculty; and university administrators. As the field of education grapples with the challenges of teacher preparation, the models of these five "lifesavers" would help to reconceptualize the profession. Exemplars such as these five teachers need to be highlighted and celebrated in teacher training curriculum. Although these five teachers may not realize just how significant their efforts were, there should be no doubt that their work with the young men in this study and others that followed may be what retained them in their profession. The successes of the five men had to be extremely rewarding for these teachers and enabled them to retain their positive approach to teaching and guiding students.

In addition to the exemplary teachers who invested significant efforts in the young men, we encountered other unsung heroes in these five life stories. We must not overlook the roles that school counselors played in several situations. It is important that we consider what K–12 counselors are involved in each and every day. Few people in a school are as in tune with the challenges of children facing difficult circumstances at home. Counselors often find themselves "on the front lines" when traumatic events occur in students' lives. They are the first to be called upon in times of crisis. Their daily schedules may be filled with a number of emergency situations in which they must address crises. They leave the school building each day with only their administrators aware of the challenges they encountered during the day. With confidentiality being critical, these professionals are seldom recognized or celebrated for their efforts. Consider the case of Dante. Without the phone call to his high school guidance counselor during the time he ran away from home, how might his experience have been different? His counselor arranged to have him return to his home community in order for the Department of Child and Protective Family Services to intervene in his family's difficult dynamics. Good school counselors invest their efforts in making children's lives better, yet they often remain unnoticed.

The responsibilities of those in counseling roles may be overwhelming; therefore, it is important that school districts implement collaborative relationships with agencies that can help young people and their families. Schools working with students from dysfunctional families must remain closely connected to community counseling centers for families and work hard to build supportive relationships with the professionals in those centers who will collaborate to guarantee that young people are safe and cared for in our communities. If we reflect on the experiences of several of the young men whose families were most dysfunctional, consider how much pain and anguish might have been prevented had interventions on the part of social workers happened sooner.

In working with families, it is important to remember Sebastian's story as a reminder of the significant role an extended family member may play in supporting a young person. Sebastian reflected on how his grandmother helped him to understand how important his education would be in assisting him to overcome his dysfunctional family's situation and create a better life for himself. His philosophical view of the world helped to ground him and reinforced his need to achieve academically. Schools must never forget to reach out to extended family members in order to help many more students like Sebastian.

The experiences of Keith, Sebastian, and Dante remind us of the importance of implementing effective anti-racist and anti-bullying programs in K–12 schools. Although these young men were fortunate to have supportive teachers who invested their efforts in them, not all teachers in their schools were as in tune with what was happening with students. When we consider how teachers were not at all aware of the bullying or gay-bashing that took place during the school day, the men's stories should serve as a call for action. As Peterson and Ray (2006) and Hinduja and Patchin (2017) noted, it is critical that teachers, coaches, and counselors be trained in detecting any bullying or gay-bashing incidents and be well equipped to professionally address incidents when they occur. Teacher, coach, and counselor preparation programs need to incorporate such training, and school districts need to maintain consistent professional development training in this area.

In addition to supportive educators, there were a number of mentors who emerged in the five life stories. The supportive adults who connected with the young men beyond their school setting only helped to reinforce the work of the emotionally supportive K–12 teachers. These adults were *naturally occurring* mentors in the lives of the five young men, similar to those found in research studies by DuBois (2005) and Hébert and Olenchak (2000). Individuals such as Keith's university debate coach, the director of Sebastian's math and science academy, and Joseph's colleague from the precollegiate engineering society for African American students highlight the value of mentors for talented students. In a mentoring relationship, shared passions, common interests, or career interests serve as the foundation of the relationship; however, the mentorships may also incorporate guidance and emotional support being passed on from mentor to protégé. These important components of the relationship will help to strengthen resilience (Castro & Zautra, 2016; Hébert, 2018a; Papházy, 2003). Humanizing relationships nurtures resilience by fostering daily moments of supportive connection with others and creating stronger sustainable social bonds that are long-lasting. Administrators, teachers, coaches, and counselors in K–12 schools and universities must consider the value of established mentoring programs from elementary school through the university years and work to build the infrastructure of such programs in their settings.

Interwoven Personal Characteristics

Evidence of the interwoven personal characteristics that shaped resilience within the men reminds us of the importance of addressing the

Conclusion

social and emotional development of gifted and talented young people in schools. Teachers, counselors, and coaches need advanced coursework and professional development programs in how to support the social and emotional well-being of our brightest students in the classroom and on the athletic field.

The men in this study benefitted from a variety of interwoven personal characteristics that supported the development of their resilience. Their perseverance, future-mindedness, practical intelligence, intensity, and empathy were traits that would benefit other young people facing difficult challenges. We can conclude that these qualities need to be celebrated. Adults who work with talented youth need to remember how important it is to call students' attention to the fact that they are equipped with these characteristics that will serve them well in their adult lives. These qualities are what will help to fill their resilience gas tank with good feelings about themselves. There is also an important need to create schools and classrooms where these resilience-boosting characteristics are nurtured and supported. Educators and counselors must consider ways in which they work together in designing psychologically safe classroom environments where psychosocial development is addressed. Such classrooms are places where students feel welcome, are comfortable sharing their authentic selves with their peers, and are supported in the development of their gifts and talents. They are places where it is okay to be intense, to express empathic feelings, to work extremely hard toward an established goal, and to focus on one's future. Models for establishing such supportive environments are provided by Baum, Schader, and Owen (2017) and Hébert (2012a, 2018b).

Theorists maintain that adults working with talented young people can actually teach the development of these beneficial personal characteristics. Teachers, counselors, coaches, and mentors can reinforce the characteristics in a variety of approaches. Schools may want to consider teaching resilience theory to talented students. Sharing biographies of talented adults who overcame serious adversity in their lives may be helpful in providing inspirational models for young people to consider. A model for this approach is described by Hébert (2009). Moreover, educators and counselors may want to share this book with their students and facilitate discussion groups with talented young men who are facing similar challenges. Another approach would include using videos, movies, or online TED talks that focus on inspirational

147

life stories. Teaching resilience theory may also be welcomed in teacher and counselor education as well as in training athletic coaches.

To nurture qualities such as perseverance, empathy, intensity, future-mindedness, and practical intelligence, educators may want to consider implementing social action projects in their schools. When talented young people become engaged in reaching out to their communities and facilitating projects that address authentic problems, they grow in many ways. Students discover outlets for their intensity and empathy. They are able to identify with others in their communities who face adversity. They are able to apply their idealism and their ability to conceptualize and address societal issues. Whether it's a "race for a cure," a spring park cleanup, or a dance marathon for a children's hospital, students discover that something can be gained by persevering, and their work helps to instill a sense of accomplishment. In carrying out social action work, they also develop supportive relationships with adults who influence how they see themselves. Successful experiences with social action projects help to build the resilience-boosting characteristics in meaningful ways (Kitano & Lewis, 2005; Price-Mitchell, 2015).

The nurturing of social and emotional development and the celebration of personal characteristics is especially important to twice-exceptional (2e) students. Patrick's experience as a 2e student should remind us of the need for counseling approaches specifically designed to address the psychosocial needs of this special population. Students like Patrick need help in coping with the stress and frustration that impacts their self-esteem and difficulties with peer relationships. They also need to understand their 2e diagnosis and learn strategies that support them in living with their disability. Patrick's experience also highlights how these challenges remain with 2e students at the university level. Learning disabilities do not simply disappear when one graduates from high school. Administrators in higher education must understand that advocacy and counseling programs for twice-exceptional students in university settings are critical for their retention and success.

Developing Talents Through Extracurricular Activities and Athletics

Educators and counselors in K–12 schools, as well as university counselors and administrators, need to pay close attention to how the talents of the young men were supported by community. The important relationships that evolved when the men connected with others who shared their interests and passions and helped shape their identities were critical to sustaining their resilience. To boost resilience in talented young people, adults who work with them need to encourage involvement in extracurricular activities and athletics. Opportunities to develop strengths beyond academics are critical. The more that school districts and institutions of higher education can do in this area, the better. Just as we saw with the men in this study, when students become involved in activities that take them to places away from their communities and enable them to see life beyond their immediate environments, they can begin to consider what life might become for them once they graduate from high school and move on to university life. Exposure to college campuses and other places and groups beyond their K–12 environments should inspire them to consider rich possibilities for the future. This future-mindedness will serve them well as young adults.

The benefits of engaging in extracurricular activities and athletics remain throughout the lifespan. Having enjoyable times with others involved in collaborative groups or teams and delving into activities that are personally meaningful can provide relief from stressors. The five men found outlets that in some ways provided them salvation from their difficult situations. Joseph's involvement in leadership, clubs, and mentoring gave him an outlet for stress relief. The same was true for Keith, who thrived on the debate teams. Sebastian found a place to "unwind" on the drill team, while Dante discovered his outlets in musical groups and running track and field. Patrick also found his salvation from his tough situation through athletics. Those experiences with stress reduction and resilience boosting will serve them well throughout adulthood and even into their golden years, as they have potential for becoming lifelong skills.

At Home in College: Finding Community and Shaping Identity

From this study, we come to understand just how significant a college experience can be to a young person who has faced adversity in adolescence. A college campus can become an oasis for a student who is arriving from a difficult home environment or has had a challenging experience in K–12 schools. Consider how Joseph entered the university as a young man removed from both parents. Keith came to the university from a family with significant problems. Sebastian and Dante both arrived on their college campus from abusive home situations, and Patrick began college after a long and difficult journey as a twice-exceptional student. With just these five young men, we see the real, diverse spectrum of tough experiences they brought with them to their college experience. With this understood, we can appreciate just how critical the collegiate experience was for propelling the lives of these young men.

What was refreshing to discover was how the men were able to put their difficulties behind them and begin a new journey. In other words, they could leave their "baggage" at home and turn the page to a new chapter in their lives. With the opportunity for a fresh new beginning, they were able to enjoy a new environment where they made new friendships with other talented students like them. As they developed their new community, they discovered a new "home" where they could explore their intellectual interests, delve into their studies, and develop their talents as they prepared for graduate school and their professional careers. Their college environments were places where the personal characteristics that boosted their resilience could be nurtured. Their university lives played a significant role in the development of their identities.

Their stories should remind K–12 and university administrators and counselors of the importance of exposing high-potential students to college campuses early in their schooling. Joseph's visit to a major university with an engineering club, Keith's field trip to an Ivy League campus for a debate competition, and Sebastian's summers in Upward Bound allowed these young men to get a sneak preview of what life could become following graduation after high school.

Just as K–12 schools across this country adapt to the changing needs of new populations of students arriving in school, colleges and universities face similar challenges. Higher education is faced with the charge of making college campuses environments where diverse student needs are addressed (Harper & Quae, 2015; Stephens, Brannon, Markus, & Nelson, 2015). Moreover, generations of students on college campuses differ in significant ways (Seemiller & Grace, 2016). The experiences of the five men highlight just how broad the spectrum of needs can be within a student body.

Universities must consider the broad spectrum of students they serve and take into account how many young people arrive on campus having survived difficult lives as young adolescents. Although students might be happy to begin a new chapter of their lives, they will need support systems in place to help them make sense of their new world and its demands. Hence, the need for counseling support systems in higher education is critical.

It is also important to remember that although students' collegiate experiences may be positive, many of the negative aspects of their lives at home continue. The adverse situations with family do not disappear. With the power of cell phone technology ever present, college students easily remain connected to their families and the ongoing drama that continues at home, whether it is a dysfunctional sibling in trouble, a family member's health challenges, or an abusive relationship that worsens. We must understand that many college students are forced to negotiate two cultures—that of higher education and the culture of their families. This can be challenging. If schools intend to retain talented students from adverse backgrounds, counseling centers and programs are critical. Ensuring that appropriate services are in place is a wise investment for the future.

Conclusion

The five talented young men overcame tough times. Resilience enabled the men to overcome problems that would overwhelm most. Their resilience was influenced by several significant factors and was strengthened over time with support from others. All of the men were fortunate to have at least one teacher who recognized their promise and invested significant personal energy and time in supporting them. Talent development opportunities during the K–12 and university years provided the men with experiences in success. The experiences with success provided them with the positive emotional feelings that allowed them to fill the "emotional gas tanks" that fueled their resilience, enabled them to cope with their stressors, helped develop important friendships, and influenced the development of their identities as talented males.

The five men benefitted from a number of interwoven personal characteristics that also supported them in developing resilience. Each of them maintained strong perseverance and displayed a sense of future-mindedness. Practical intelligence contributed to their survival and success. They also benefitted from their intensity and having a sense of empathy.

When they entered college, they enjoyed their new independence and continued their work in developing their talents. Finding outlets for talent development in high-powered academic courses, athletic teams, musical groups, and leadership and social action projects, they were able to see themselves as capable men who could thrive intellectually, athletically, and socially. This success enabled them to view themselves as talented men capable of moving on to enjoy lives of accomplishment and fulfillment.

AFTERWORD

My Message to Joseph, Keith, Sebastian, Dante, and Patrick

Gentlemen, as I conclude this book, I realize there is no way that I can adequately thank you for your participation in this research. You gave me your time and shared your life stories with generosity and humility. You were gracious in allowing me to spend quality time engaged in conversations that may have been painful for you at times. My hope is that this experience was in some way therapeutic. I am honored to have had the opportunity to capture your stories. Our work together has influenced my life in many positive ways. I will always remain indebted to you. My hope is that I have shared your stories with my readers in such ways that will help to pass on important lessons of resilience. As a result, many more talented young men who face adversity will be helped.

As you read this message, know how pleased I was to be able to share with my readers your personal and professional successes in the epilogue of each chapter. I am proud of your achievements and celebrate what you have done with your lives since our time together. Your stories are inspirational and should encourage others to persevere, remain focused on their goals, and enjoy lives of fulfillment. Lastly, know that you are always in my heart.

Warmly,

Tom

REFERENCES

Ahern, N. R., Ark, P., & Byers, J. (2008). Resilience and coping strategies in adolescents. *Pediatric Nursing, 20*(10), 32–36.

Batson, C. D., Ahmad, N., Lishner, D. A., & Tsang, J. (2002). Empathy and altruism. In C. R. Snyder & S. J. Lopez (Eds.), *Handbook of positive psychology* (pp. 485–498). New York, NY: Oxford University Press.

Baum, S. M., Schader, R. M., & Owen, S. V. (2017). *To be gifted and learning disabled: Strength-based strategies for helping twice-exceptional students with LD, ADHD, ASD, and more* (3rd ed.). Waco, TX: Prufrock Press.

Beckerman, N. L. (2017). LGBT teens and bullying: What every social worker should know. *Mental Health in Family Medicine, 13,* 486–494.

Boniwell, I. (2006). *Positive psychology in a nutshell.* London, England: PWBC.

Bridges, E. M. (2013). "Back in the day, man, I wish someone would have told me like it really is": Liberatory education for gifted African Americans. In T. C. Grantham, M. F. Trotman Scott, & D. A. Harmon (Eds.). *Young, triumphant, and Black: Overcoming the tyranny of segregated minds in desegregated schools* (pp. 333–339). Waco, TX: Prufrock Press.

Bucknavage, L. B., & Worrell, F. C. (2005). A study of academically talented students' participation in extracurricular activities. *Journal of Secondary Gifted Education, 16,* 74–86.

Calvert, E., & Cleveland, E. (2006). Extracurricular activities. In F. A. Dixon & S. M. Moon (Eds.), *The handbook of secondary gifted education* (pp. 527–546). Waco, TX: Prufrock Press.

Cassell, E. J. (2002). Compassion. In C. R. Snyder & S. J. Lopez (Eds.), *Handbook of positive psychology* (pp. 434–445). New York, NY: Oxford University Press.

Castro, S. A., & Zautra, A. J. (2016). Humanization of social relations: Nourishing health and resilience through greater humanity. *Journal of Theoretical and Philosophical Psychology, 36,* 64–80.

DuBois, D. L. (2005). Natural mentoring relationships and adolescent health: Evidence from a national study. American *Journal of Public Health, 95,* 518–524.

Duckworth, A. (2016). *Grit: The power of passion and perseverance.* New York, NY: Scribner.

Duckworth, A. L., Peterson, C., Matthews, M. D., Kelly, D. R. (2007). Grit: Perseverance and passion for long-term goals. *Journal of Personality and Social Psychology, 92,* 1087–1101.

Fiske, S. T. (2009). *Social beings: Core motives in social psychology.* New York, NY: John Wiley.

Flowers, R. B. (2010). *Street kids: The lives of runaway and throwaway teens.* Jefferson, NC: McFarland & Company.

Friedrichs, T. (2018). Educating gifted gay, lesbian, bisexual, transgender, and questioning students. In J. L. Roberts, T. F. Inman, & J. H. Robins (Eds.), *Introduction to gifted education.* (pp. 387–398). Waco, TX: Prufrock Press.

Gallagher, M. W. (2009). Future mindedness. In S. J. Lopez (Ed.). *The encyclopedia of positive psychology* (2nd ed., pp. 418–420). Hoboken, NJ: Wiley-Blackwell.

Gould, D., Collins, K., Lauer, L., & Chung, Y. (2007). Coaching life skills through football: A study of award winning high school coaches. *Journal of Applied Sport Psychology, 19,* 16–37.

Greenspon, T. S. (2012). *Moving past perfect: How perfectionism may be holding back your kids (and you!) and what you can do about it.* Minneapolis, MN: Free Spirit.

Haidt, J. (2006). *The happiness hypothesis: Putting ancient wisdom and philosophy to the test of modern science.* London, England: Arrow.

Harper, S. R., & Quae, S. J. (2015). Making engagement equitable for students in U.S. higher education. In S. J. Quae & S. R. Harper (Eds.), *Student engagement in higher education: Theoretical perspectives and practical approaches for diverse populations* (2nd ed., pp. 1–14). New York, NY: Routledge.

Heath, S. B., & McLaughlin, M. W. (1993). *Identity and inner-city youth: Beyond ethnicity and gender.* New York, NY: Teachers College Press.

Hébert, T. P. (1995). Coach Brogan: South Central High School's answer to academic achievement. *Journal of Secondary Gifted Education, 7,* 310–323.

Hébert, T. P. (2000). Defining belief in self: Intelligent young men in an urban high school. *Gifted Child Quarterly, 44,* 91–114.

Hébert, T. P. (2002). Gifted Black males in a predominantly White university: Portraits of achievement. *Journal for the Education of the Gifted, 26,* 25–64.

Hébert, T. P. (2006). Gifted university males in a Greek fraternity: Creating a culture of achievement. *Gifted Child Quarterly, 50,* 26–41.

Hébert, T. P. (2009). Guiding gifted teenagers to self-understanding through biography. In J. VanTassel-Baska, T. L. Cross, & F. R. Olenchak (Eds.), *Social-emotional curriculum for gifted students* (pp. 259–287). Waco, TX: Prufrock Press.

Hébert, T. P. (2011). *Understanding the social and emotional lives of gifted students.* Waco, TX: Prufrock Press.

Hébert, T. P. (2012a). Creating classroom environments for social and emotional development. In S. K. Johnsen (Ed.), *NAGC Pre-K-Grade 12 gifted education programming standards: A guide to planning and implementing high-quality services* (pp. 27–44). Waco, TX: Prufrock Press.

Hébert, T. P. (2012b). Addressing the counseling needs of gifted boys. In T. L. Cross & J. Riedel Cross (Eds.), *Handbook for counselors serving students with gifts and talents: Development, relationships, school issues, and counseling needs/interventions* (pp. 333–350). Waco, TX: Prufrock Press.

Hébert, T. P. (2013). Gifted males: Understanding their challenges and honoring their potential. In C. M. Callahan & H. Hertberg-Davis (Eds.), *Fundamentals of gifted education* (pp. 331–343). New York, NY: Routledge Press.

Hébert, T. P. (2018a). An examination of high-achieving first-generation college students from low-income backgrounds. *Gifted Child Quarterly, 62*,1–15.

Hébert, T. P. (2018b). Designing the learning environment for gifted students. In J. L. Roberts, T. F. Inman, & J. H. Robins (Eds.), *Introduction to gifted education* (pp. 183–195). Waco, TX: Prufrock Press.

Hébert, T. P., & Olenchak, F. R. (2000). Mentors for gifted, underachieving males: Developing potential and realizing promise. *Gifted Child Quarterly, 44*, 196–207.

Hébert, T. P., & Reis, S. M. (1999). Culturally diverse high-achieving students in an urban high school. *Urban Education, 34*, 428–457.

Hinduja, S., & Patchin, J. W. (2017). Cultivating youth resilience to prevent bullying and cyberbullying victimization. *Child Abuse & Neglect, 73*, 51–62.

Howes, L. (2017). *The mask of masculinity: How men can embrace vulnerability, create strong relationships, and live their fullest lives.* New York, NY: Rodale.

Johnson, E. I., & Easterling, B. A. (2015). Coping with confinement: Adolescents' experiences with parental incarceration. *Journal of Adolescent Research, 30*, 244–267.

Kitano, M. K., & Lewis, R. B. (2005). Resilience and coping: Implications for gifted children and youth at risk. *Roeper Review, 27*, 200–205.

Leiber, J., & Stoller, M. (1969). Is that all there is? [Recorded by Peggy Lee]. On *Is that all there is?* [Record album]. Los Angeles, CA: Capitol Records.

Lipkin, A. (2001). *Understanding homosexuality, changing schools.* New York, NY: Routledge.

Maddox, S. J. (2013). Ain't that peculiar: Gifted, Black, and male overcoming the fourth grade failure syndrome. In T. C. Grantham, M. F. Trotman Scott, & D. A. Harmon (Eds.), *Young, triumphant, and Black: Overcoming the tyranny of segregated minds in desegregated schools* (pp. 63–68). Waco, TX: Prufrock Press.

Martinez, R. J. (2006). Understanding runaway teens. *Journal of Child and Adolescent Psychiatric Nursing, 19,* 77–88.

Masten, A. S., & Reed, M. J. (2002). Resilience in development. In C. R. Snyder & S. J. Lopez (Eds.), *Handbook of positive psychology* (pp. 74–88). New York, NY: Oxford University Press.

Neenan, M. (2018). *Developing resilience: A cognitive-behavioral approach.* (2nd ed.). New York, NY: Routledge.

Neihart, M. (2002). Risk and resilience in gifted children: A conceptual framework. In M. Neihart, S. M. Reis, N. M. Robinson, & S. M. Moon (Eds.), *The social and emotional development of gifted children: What do we know?* (pp. 113–122). Waco, TX: Prufrock Press.

Newman, R. (2003). In the wake of disaster: Building the resilience initiative of APA's public education campaign. In E. H. Grotberg (Ed.), *Resilience for today: Gaining strength from adversity* (pp. 211–240). Westport, CT: Praeger.

Olszewski-Kubilius, P., & Lee, S. (2004). The role of participation in in-school and outside-of-school activities in the talent development of gifted students. *Journal of Secondary Gifted Education, 15,* 107–123.

O'Neil, J. M. (2015). *Men's gender role conflict: Psychological costs, consequences, and an agenda for change.* Washington, DC: American Psychological Association.

Papházy, J. E. (2003). Resilience, the fourth R: The role of schools in this promotion. In E. H. Grotberg (Ed.), *Resilience for today: Gaining strength from adversity* (pp. 105–140). Westport, CT: Praeger.

Park, S., & Schepp, K. G. (2015). A systematic review of research on children of alcoholics: Their inherent resilience and vulnerability. *Journal of Child and Family Studies, 24,* 1222–1231.

Peterson, J. S. (1997). Bright, tough, and resilient—and not in a gifted program. *The Journal of Secondary Education, 8,* 121–136.

Peterson, J. S., & Ray, K. E. (2006). Bullying and the gifted: Victims, perpetrators, prevalence, and effects. *Gifted Child Quarterly, 50,* 148–168.

Piechowski, M. M. (2013). *"Mellow out," they say, if only I could: Intensities and sensitivities of the young and bright (2nd ed.).* Unionville, NY: Royal Fireworks Press.

Price-Mitchell, M. (2015). *Tomorrow's change makers: Reclaiming the power of citizenship for a new generation.* Bainbridge Island, WA: Eagle Harbor Publishing.

Reis, S. M., Colbert, R., & Hébert, T. P. (2005). Understanding resilience in diverse, talented students in an urban high school. *Roeper Review, 27,* 110–120.

Rotter, J. B. (1990). Internal versus external control of reinforcement: A case history of a variable. *American Psychologist, 45,* 489–493.

Roy, A. L., McCoy, D. C., & Raver, C. C. (2014). Instability versus quality: Residential mobility, neighborhood poverty, and children's self-regulation. *Developmental Psychology, 50,* 1891–1896.

Scarf, D., Moradi, S., McGaw, K., Hewitt, J., Hayhurst, J. G., Boyes, M., . . . Hunter. J. A. (2016). Somewhere I belong: Long-term increases in adolescents' resilience are predicted by perceived belonging to the in-group. *British Journal of Social Psychology, 55,* 588–599.

Schuler, P. (2000). Perfectionism and the gifted adolescent. *Journal of Secondary Gifted Education, 11,* 183–196.

Seemiller, C., & Grace, M. (2016). *Generation Z goes to college.* San Francisco, CA: Jossey-Bass.

Sheldon, K. M., & Bettencourt, B. (2002). Psychological need-satisfaction and subjective well-being within social groups. *British Journal of Social Psychology, 41,* 25–38.

Shelton, S., & Barnes, M. (2016). "Racism just isn't an issue anymore": Preservice teachers' resistances to the intersections of sexuality and race. *Teaching and Teacher Education, 55,* 165–174.

Stephens, N. M., Brannon, T. N., Markus, H. R., & Nelson, J. E. (2015). Feeling at home in college: Fortifying school-relevant selves to reduce social class disparities in higher education. *Social Issues and Policy Review, 9,* 1–24.

Sternberg, R. J., Forsythe, G. B., Hedlund, J., Horvath, J. A., Wagner, R. K., Williams, W. M., . . . Grigorenko, E. L. (2000). *Practical intelligence in everyday life.* New York, NY: Cambridge University Press.

Werner, E. E. (2015). Resilience research: Past, present, and future. In R. D. Peters, B. Leadbeater, & R. McMahon (Eds.), *Resilience in children, families, and communities: Linking context to practice and policy,* (pp. 3–11). Boston, MA: Springer.

References

Williams, J. M., Bryan, J., Morrison, S., & Scott, T. R. (2017). Protective factors and processes contributing to the academic success of students living in poverty: Implications for counselors. *Journal of Multicultural Counseling and Development, 45,* 183–200.

Zimmerman, M. A., Stoddard, S. A., Eisman, A. B., Caldwell, C. H., Aiyer, S. M., & Miller, A. (2013). Adolescent resilience: Promotive factors that inform prevention. *Child Development Perspectives, 7*(4), 1–9.

ABOUT THE AUTHOR

Thomas P. Hébert, Ph.D., is Professor of Gifted and Talented Education in the College of Education at the University of South Carolina. He has more than a decade of K–12 classroom experience working with gifted students and 25 years in higher education training graduate students and educators in gifted education. He has also conducted research for the National Research Center on the Gifted and Talented (NRC/GT). He served on the Board of Directors of the National Association for Gifted Children (NAGC). He has served as a consultant to schools nationally and internationally in Italy, Taiwan, Paraguay, Peru, Mexico, Colombia, Chile, Ghana, and Hong Kong.

Dr. Hébert's research interests include social and emotional development of gifted students, culturally diverse gifted students, and problems gifted young men face. He is the author of the award-winning text *Understanding the Social and Emotional Lives of Gifted Students*. Dr. Hébert has received numerous research and teaching awards, including the 2000 Early Scholar Award from NAGC and the 2012 Distinguished Alumni Award from the Neag School of Education at the University of Connecticut.